GOD
Will ARISE

A Biblical Validation of Inner Healing

ANDREW W GOTT

WESTBOW
PRESS®
A DIVISION OF THOMAS NELSON
& ZONDERVAN

WestBow Press books may be ordered through booksellers or by contacting:

WestBow Press
A Division of Thomas Nelson & Zondervan
1663 Liberty Drive
Bloomington, IN 47403
www.westbowpress.com
844-714-3454

ISBN: 978-1-6642-6827-2 (sc)
ISBN: 978-1-6642-6826-5 (hc)
ISBN: 978-1-6642-6828-9 (e)

Library of Congress Control Number: 2022910626

Print information available on the last page.

WestBow Press rev. date: 07/13/2022

CONTENTS

PREFACE

BEFORE DELVING INTO THE SCRIPTURES CONCERNING THIS redemptive concept, it is necessary to step back and locate the intention and purpose of this validating work. In the span of over three decades that have passed since God initiated me into inner healing, I have read and heard great discussions from both sides of the aisle. One side says that the principles are throughout the Word of God. The other side is convinced that the principles are far away from the truth of Scripture and is merely a form of charismatic psychology. Knowing that God is not the author of confusion (1 Corinthians 14:33), I personally made a quality decision to sit down before the Word of God to find out what the Word itself had to say concerning the matter. The result of that effort is this writing, which I do not believe is a truly exhaustive search but is merely a fundamental explanation of the ministry.

The purpose, therefore, is to scripturally show the validity of the inner healing principles as a work of the Spirit of God that He will confirm with signs following. God is not known for supporting principles and concepts that are contrary to His revealed character and will in the Word, but He will confirm His Word (Mark 16:20). A course or path of intensive studying to show yourself approved unto God (2 Timothy 2:15) is a useful source of information for a Word-validation such as this. Also, it is my conviction that I have a transformed inner man as a resource of information. Although God's redemptive work in us continues, I believe that major aspects of my inner life are producing the fruit of God as a product of His plowing, planting, and harvesting in my life throughout these years.

In addition to any ministry work becoming successful and showing lasting fruit, it is imperative that the other parts of the recipient's life show an inclination toward obedience to God and a reliance on the Word of God. This is because inner healing prayer is by no means a cure-all or quick way to freedom. I believe it to be just one piece of the mystery of God, the plan of redemption (1 Corinthians 2:7, Colossians 2:2). It is one brick that God is building on the foundational stone of Jesus Christ. Without the continuation of personal study of the Word of God, praying in the Spirit, hearing solid preaching, and all the other spiritual exercises and disciplines of Christian fellowship, our healing will be incomplete, or we may allow the thief to steal the seed of this word of healing and transformation from our hearts. Jesus urged the leper who He had just cleansed to fulfill the requirements of the law (Matthew 8:4).

Our commitment to the Lord must also be secure, because inner healing can be getting into the thick of the battle with our old self and with the enemy. Long-held territory is not easily returned as spoil. Our commitment must be strong, in order that we do not become double-minded and wavering in the heat of the battle. During this season, we need to understand that this trial of our faith, which in this instance is the believing that God has ministered deliverance to us and has set our emotions free, is much more precious than gold. After standing against the attack of the enemy, we will be able to walk in the freedom and glory that follow, producing the fruit of a preserved soul.

I

That the Scripture Might Be Fulfilled

TRUE PROPHETIC UTTERANCE WILL EVENTUALLY COME TO PASS within the earth, and the prophetic Word of God is to be taken seriously. Since God's purpose is to reveal His secrets to His prophets, a specific doctrine or principle will have been prophesied centuries before the actual moving of the Spirit of God within these realms. Samuel prophesied the recreation of the human spirit (born again) in 1 Samuel 10:6, which Ezekiel confirmed in Ezekiel 11:19. The triumphant return of the Lord Jesus Christ is prophesied in 1 Thessalonians 4:15–17. The rest and comfort of the Holy Spirit to the believer through speaking in tongues was prophesied in Isaiah 28:11–12. Most New Testament doctrine can be located within the writings of the Old Testament.

Like those other doctrines, the ministry of inner healing was prophesied about many years before its current restoration within the church. As it is with other doctrines as well, there seems to be a specific set time for the manifestation to become prominent. In noticing the signs of our times, we can thank God for the pinpoint accuracy of the Spirit of God. The numbers of unwanted children and divorce continue to stifle the influence of the family and can cause rejection to be a heart stimulus within a generation or culture.

1

Occult involvement is no longer limited to the bored or outcasts of society, as hypnosis continues to be a prevalent activity. Jesus even spoke in Luke 21:26 of this time as one that would be characterized with dominating fear and a loss of emotional control. The Greek word translated "heart" in the King James of that verse is the Greek word *psuche*, or soul. No ability to control your mind, will or emotions because of fear. In 2 Timothy 3, the apostle Paul through the Holy Spirit prophetically listed as a sign of the last days a growth in abuse and violence, which perfectly characterizes our current abusive and violent generation. The Spirit of God knew what He was doing in bringing about the restoration of the inner healing prayer ministry in this specific generation. Praise God for His foreknowledge and for His concern about His children.

This principle of prophetic fulfillment is personified in the person of Jesus Christ, Who is the fulfillment of Old Testament promises through His life, death, and resurrection. In Matthew 5:17, He declared that He came to fulfill both the law and the prophets. In Luke 4:21, Jesus declared the prophecy of Isaiah 61 fulfilled that day because of His presence there and the anointing of the Spirit He had received at His baptism. Some of us are waiting for heaven to inherit blessings when the finished work of Jesus Christ has made a way for certain blessings to be operative in our lives today. The baptism of the Holy Spirit is a fulfillment of the Feast of first fruits (Romans 8:23, Exodus 23:16).

Concisely, inner healing can be classified as the Spirit of counsel with the supernatural manifestation of the gifts of healings (1 Corinthians 12:9). Grammatically, this is accurate, because the words "gifts," which is *charisma* in the Greek, and "healings" are found in their plural form in the original text. This not only implies there are specific physical healing anointings, but that the plurality also speaks about specific anointings for soulish and emotional weaknesses. This healing deals with the types of wounds that are rooted in the subconscious area of the soul and heart through the healing power of the Holy Spirit. During the outpouring of the soul, the Spirit of God will manifest Himself in the gifts of healings, bringing His healing power to minister about a specific event or situation that He wants to deal with. To put it another way, inner healing prayer is counseling under the anointing of God, "that same anointing that teaches you of all things, and is truth, and is no lie" (1 John 2:27, KJV). The anointing is the only thing with the necessary power to break the yoke of bondage (Isaiah 10:27). Natural wisdom, knowledge, and psychological insight have limitations and are finite, whereas our ultimate faith should be in the power of God and His love and grace for His children. The Scriptures in these analyzed paragraphs will show Jesus in the work of inner healing and the restoration of broken hearts.

Malachi 4:1–3

> For behold, the day cometh, that shall burn as an oven; and all the proud, yea, and all that do wickedly, shall be stubble: and the day that cometh shall burn them up, saith the Lord of hosts, that it shall leave them neither root nor branch. But unto you that fear my name shall the Sun of righteousness arise with healing in His wings; and ye shall go forth, and grow up as calves of the stall. And ye shall tread down the wicked; for they shall be ashes under the soles of your feet in the day that I shall do this, saith the Lord of hosts. (KJV)

In this world of myriad views and opinions, God has many of His own as well. He is patiently waiting for His people to live with greater unity. When we are seeking greater dimensions of God or He is doing a sanctifying work in our lives, He will brood over these new revelations so they can come into full effect.

A glorious example of this happened to me when the Lord was beginning to give me the revelation of this prophetic word. I had been through a few healing prayer sessions, was rejoicing because of new-found freedom, and I was growing closer to the Lord. During this same time, the enemy had a plan to try and steal this word out of my heart. Early growth is sensitive to attack at these times and a book came across my path that denounced all these newfound concepts. From this place of questioning, I was going to receive ministry in a few days. Thankfully, the Holy Spirit is aware. As my friend/prayer partner and I went back to his office, and I sat down, the Lord spoke very clearly in my heart, "The Sun of righteousness will arise with healing in His wings." I had read that verse before but did not have real familiarity with it. My spirit rejoiced from the power of that word. As we got into prayer, Roy said these words: "We thank You, Lord, that these past things are under Your Blood, and are forgiven, but we thank You also that You have come to heal the hurts and wounds." The seed of doubt tried to diminish the need of this type of prayer for the believer while I was learning that inner healing prayer can promote resurrection life. Bringing up sin promotes death and burial, but it is vital to gently expose wounds associated with the sin and move upward toward resurrection. Tears filled my eyes in that moment as I realized the amazing accuracy and concern of my Father.

In getting back to the prophetic word from Malachi, let us notice that there is a specific day, a certain set time for all this to take place. As Jesus told His mother at the wedding in Cana of Galilee, "Mine hour is not yet come," so many things of God have specific set schedules. Obviously, the set time originates on the Day of Pentecost, the birthday of the kingdom and the church. The early church lived in the authority that Jesus had given them. But, because of religion and the Dark Ages, there has been a necessary work of restoration of the ways of the Spirit of God back in the church. That has been going on for hundreds of years since the Reformation. Appropriating the healing virtue of the presence of the Lord Jesus to hearts and minds is one of these things God is restoring. Before this specific restoration, other things had to come first. The manifestations of the Spirit in operation and the Word of God as final authority were a necessary foundation. As we begin to attack enemy strongholds, some that have been operating for years and generations, we must have our swords sharpened and ready for battle. After this, God began to prepare the hearts of the prayer warriors. It takes great love and patience to spend time counseling with people and great compassion to listen to shame-filled experiences that maybe no one else will ever hear. Thank God for those people who have heard the Shepherd's voice. With all the preceding layers secured, it was again the set time to bring forth this word of restoration.

"It shall leave them neither root nor branch." These words prophesy about one of the effects of this day of healing. We can easily look at our lives as trees. We produce fruit for either God or the enemy. God plants a seed into our lives, called the incorruptible seed, the Word of God. The enemy also tries to plant a seed, called corruptible seed. As children, we can be limited in our defense against attacks, thereby being destroyed for a lack of knowledge. Children desperately need the spiritual covering of a godly father and mother to stand up for them against these times. Over the years, this corruptible seed can grow into plants that have deep roots and branches that cause believers to act ungodly or say poisonous things. Everyone is tempted with a thought to do wrong but having limited power to bring the thought captive or doing the action is the evil fruit of the corruptible seed. These actions can then produce a demonic root of rejection, resentment, or fear in our lives. If these roots grew from events in our childhood, we may be unaware of them except for the evil fruit they still produce in our lives. As in the natural, roots many times can be seen only by the process of digging into the ground to expose them. When there are excessive amounts of erosion, everyone can see them. These erosion people are severely tormented, unable to function properly in society and life. But the roots that need exposure can be just as deadly. Only the Lord knows the events in our past that have caused wounds and as we submit to His Spirit, He will begin His work. To begin, we need to have hearing ears. If He exposes, but we resist, it will not work. One of the best ways to allow the Spirit to search is to pray in tongues so that He that searches the hearts can make intercession for us, because we know not what we should pray for (paraphrase of Romans 8:26–27). As we receive healing, the roots and branches of the corruptible seed are removed.

Exposure can feel like death and burial; yet now we need healing to experience His resurrection power. Malachi prophesied that the Sun of righteousness, Jesus Christ, will arise to do this. Not only is the enemy rooted out, but we can also reestablish authority in our life and possess the land. With the healing, we can really believe that Jehovah-Jireh is our provider and the judgmental attitude toward our lack has been rooted out. Parents give an abundance of material things to their kids. Are they giving out of an attitude of love and reward for their children or out of resentment toward their childhood situation? In working hard to give all these material things to their own children, are they forgetting to give the things their children need most, like love and security? Roots of resentment and lack can be generational.

The purpose of inner healing is growing up into maturity, as stated in verse two: "and ye shall go forth, and grow up as calves of the stall." As the roots of wickedness are cut off, we can grow into green olive trees in the house of the Lord. Our renewed lives can provide shade and fruit for others to see and grow. Our victorious life will be the ashes of the enemy under our feet. Matthew 18 speaks to these inner healing concepts, from offending little ones, the presence of Jesus where two or three are gathered (prayer partner) and the power of agreement prayer.

Zechariah 13:1–2

> In that day there shall be a fountain opened to the house of David and to the inhabitants of Jerusalem for sin and for uncleanness. And it shall come to pass in that day, saith the Lord of hosts, I will cut off the names of the idols out of the land, and they shall no more be remembered; and also I will cause the

prophets and the unclean spirit to pass out of the land. (KJV)

Through my studies within the Word of God, it has become increasingly evident of the need to define terms from their original Hebrew or Greek words. Without this, we can limit the effect of the Word because of the limited English language and the era and the knowledge of the translators. I believe that much of the strife and division within God's people could be diminished by intensive original language studies. For example, one of the Hebrew words for praise can mean to extend the hand; another can mean to be clamorously foolish. This implies that praise to God can be interactive and loud. This verse in Zechariah becomes clearer by using this study principle.

In verse one, there are two words that can be further translated and analyzed. "Fountain," in the beginning of the verse refers to a source or supply, and is the same Hebrew word used in Jeremiah 2:13 describing the Holy Spirit as the Fountain of Living Waters. "Uncleanness" is not a poor translation, but the phrase can be broadened. The proper usage of the word signifies rejection, moral impurity and impurity through incest or idolatry. It is used in Leviticus 20:21 where God speaks of the taking of your brother's wife as an unclean thing. This verse in Zechariah speaks to me of a specific day of restoration where the Holy Spirit will be a supply of healing for His people from the effects of rejection in general, but specifically for rejection caused through moral impurity. God is prophesying of a specific anointing to minister to the rejected, the incest victims, and those oppressed by idolatrous practices and occult involvement. This area can include those affected by child abuse, sexual abuse, and physical abuse. These events can create demonic bondage and soul ties that oppress a person throughout life. Special miracles may cause demons to leave without prayer warfare (Acts 19:11–12), but normally warfare and working by the Spirit will be needed. The last part of verse two deals with the teamwork part of deliverance within inner healing prayer: "I will cause the unclean spirit to pass out of the land." Deliverance may not always be required, but I believe that any ministry in the Spirit has this potential. Personally, I received ministry that was simply prayer and confession, other times it involved greater warfare. This ministry also is vital for those involved with occult and cult groups. Strong leaders in cult groups can display extreme control over their followers and sexual ties from deviant practices can produce soul ties that hinder a person from being able to flow with God or others. These memories can be healed so that the words of Zechariah can be fulfilled in the life of a believer.

Isaiah 30:25–26

> And there shall be upon every high mountain and upon every high hill, rivers and streams of water in the day of the great slaughter, when the towers fall. Moreover, the light of the moon shall be as the light of the sun, and the light of the sun shall be sevenfold, as the light of seven days in the day that the Lord bindeth up the breach of His people, and healeth the stroke of their wounds. (KJV)

This prophetic word speaks of a specific time where there are cleansing streams and rivers along with increasing glory or light that correlate to a working of God to bind up hearts and heal wounds. Isaiah prophesied that even the high hills will not be able to escape the flow of the cleansing tide of this work. The apostle Paul spoke about the "high thing that exalts itself against the knowledge of God" in 2 Corinthians 10:5 (KJV), which can fit into this concept as well. He spoke of these things in the context of engaging in spiritual warfare and the victory over strongholds. The other aspect of Isaiah's prophecy is the increasing intensity of the light of God within this prophetic event. We all have aspects of darkness in our character and personalities that need the light of God to show us clearly our true nature. As God's people abide closer to Him, this light can intensify. The children of Israel were afraid of this closeness, but Jesus encouraged us to come to the light so that our deeds can be clearly seen (John 3:21).

Prophetic Summary

Over thirty times in the Gospels, we read the phrase, "that the Scripture might be fulfilled." Jesus Christ is the personal fulfillment of the promises of God. In Matthew 5:17, He told the multitude that He came to fulfill the law and the prophets. The promises of restoration in these preceding verses can be fulfilled in your life by receiving this working of God within your heart and soul. Amos 3:7 says, "surely the Lord God will do nothing but He revealeth His secrets unto His servants the prophets" (KJV). Malachi, Zechariah, and Isaiah all seem to point to a specific time of restoration where God will be bringing healing, spiritual maturity, rivers of refreshing and increasing intensity of His presence. These words speak to many of the concepts and principles of inner healing prayer and the working of God's healing through the Spirit of counsel and might. We can have tremendous revelation and still be blind to other dimensions of God. Peter had the revelation of Jesus as the Messiah and Son of God (Matthew 16:16–17) but could not yet see clearly about His suffering and death (Matthew 16:21–23). If you have the revelation of deliverance, begin to receive the prophetic word of restoration concerning inner healing as it helps produce the relationship between Jesus and the individual by allowing the Lord to specifically manifest Himself and show His true nature to His children.

II

A Logos Defense

SINCE THE TIME OF THE FALL OF HUMANITY, GOD HAS ALWAYS SEEMED to have to deal with the critic. The enemy thought that he could do a better job than the Creator and manipulated His instructions. Adam rebelled and tried to blame God for giving him his helper. Jesus constantly ran into and confronted the ultimate critic, the Pharisee. Although some do not believe, that does not make the faith of God useless (paraphrase of Romans 3:3). In fact, the opposite happens. When Jesus was crucified, the Trinity were the only ones who genuinely believed in what Jesus had spoken so much about, the resurrection. When the world system is overwhelmed in unbelief, God says, "all things are possible to him that believeth" (Mark 9:23, KJV).

In the realm of inner healing concepts, the critics have risen as well. In 1 Peter 3:15, the Holy Spirit urges us to "always be ready to give a logical defense to anyone who asks you to account for the hope that is in you, but do it courteously and respectfully" (Amplified Bible). In that translation, the word "account" has the Greek word *logos* as its root. Therefore, Peter is admonishing believers that we need to be able to prove, through the Word of God, the reason for our confidence.

Effects of the Past

Critics have articulated issues with any principle that suggests an essential time of ministry for analyzing and exposing past emotional wounds and hurts as merely charismatic psychology. Yet, a parallel principle of the Spirit of God exposing darkness is also an essential part of the new birth process. The conviction of the Spirit, within a specific time or ongoing process, is what causes the unbeliever to recognize their sin and their drastic need for a Savior. A person can feel proud and strong one minute, but when the convicting power of the Spirit comes upon them, their cry is "what must I do to be saved"? The darkness and the need were always there, but God begins to show us the truth of our rebellion in the presence of a holy God. Although the unbeliever may have sat through hours of good preaching and years of witnessing, when the Spirit moves graciously it becomes a reckoning moment of decision in their life.

Likewise, it can take a specific moving of the Spirit upon us to show a believer the dark areas of their life that are frustrating the reign of their born-anew spirit. This principle realizes our triune nature and the characteristics and uniqueness of each part of the human being; namely, spirit, soul, and body. Positionally, our spirit has been recreated and is perfect, but Peter implied that the complete salvation of the soul comes at the end or conclusion of faith (1 Peter 1:9). This signifies a continual and consistent working of God throughout the life of the believer. The full redemption of the body happens at the resurrection. This idea of darkness within the soul of the believer is also brought forth in 1 John 1:8; "if we say that we have no sin, we deceive ourselves, and the truth is not in us" (KJV). This is from the same apostle and book that teaches that whosoever is born of God cannot sin (1 John 3:9). This is not contradictory when you understand the distinction between soul and spirit. Jeremiah 17 also speaks of this principle by declaring the truly deceitful, wicked nature of the heart and God beginning a work of searching it out and trying the heart to purify it.

In the book of Lamentations, Jeremiah reiterates this concept. In

Lamentations 3:19–20, it is written; "O Lord, remember earnestly my affliction and my misery, my wandering and my outcast state, the wormwood and the gall. My soul has them continually in remembrance, and is bowed down within me" (Amplified Bible). The soul can be easily burdened and depressed. Although it is possible to be a mighty warrior on our own, this oppression may need the wisdom and encouragement of a prayer partner and friend to help us see victory. The prophet spoke about the answer to his dilemma in verses forty and forty-one: "Let us test and examine our ways and let us return to the Lord. Let us lift up our hearts and hands and then with them mount up in prayer to God in heaven" (Amplified Bible).

The psychological redemption of the soul of a human seems to follow the same pattern of the restoration of all things through a process of time and greater levels of glory. Our world today is still affected by the fall of humanity and the entrance of sin, even though it was thousands of years ago. Jesus Christ has come and paid the price for redemption, but our world still walks in darkness until the restitution of all things. In parallel, our past can affect our behavior today, even if we have been born anew. The finality of His work is complete, but we must learn how to appropriate the promises and work out His sanctifying process that will culminate in the conclusion of our faith. The earth will see its culmination at His triumphant return to set up His kingdom.

What is the Subconscious?

The Word of God uses different terms to identify the complicated nature of a human person. Translations can be inaccurate in using these terms or have redundancy in their use that is incomplete. The word "heart" is one that is used in dominance and has been correlated with the human spirit. Yet, by both the Hebrew and Greek definitions, the words translated "heart" mean the feelings and thoughts within the center of our being. These characteristics are more commonly linked to the soulish realm of a person. In Hebrews 4:12, it speaks of the sharpness of the sword of the Word that distinguishes between the specific actions of the soul and spirit. Yet, it also speaks to this sharpness as a discerner, a judge, of the thoughts and intents of the heart. Is this implying that this could be an even deeper breakdown into the heart and soul of a person? Human understanding and insight would be limited in this realm.

The subconscious is this realm of the heart where the true purposes and motives reside. Throughout the Scriptures, we are taught that God tries the heart, examines the hearts, to show the true character. That is because the human being has learned to act deceptively and to disregard true feelings to avoid confrontation or trouble. We may say that we keep it inside or in the back of our mind. However, it still affects us. Under circumstantial pressure or emotional adverse conditions, these true feelings can rise to the surface and show out. Another term used in the Scripture says that God knows the secrets of the heart. This term speaks specifically to this subconscious realm. Secrets of the heart – secrets in our emotions, our feelings, our inmost thoughts. Things that make people cry or be anxious for no apparent reason. Sudden violent behavior in someone who has had no manifested history of such acts. Those secret feelings of bitterness and anger that we hold in while we are in the company of that person, while we stand tormented, stomach in knots, full of confusion. This area is not hidden from God, though. In fact, He seems to want to expose some of these things, in His timing, in His grace. In Revelation 2:23, He said: "I am He who searches minds, the thoughts, feelings, and purposes and the inmost hearts" (Amplified Bible). In Psalms 51:6, King David asked for wisdom in his hidden, inmost heart. Psalms 28:3 speaks of people who speak peace to neighbors, but malice and mischief are in their hearts. The Psalms have many verses that speak of praising God with your whole heart – transforming our inmost heart to learn how to receive from God.

In 1 Corinthians 2:10–11, Paul shares a spiritual exercise that can be worked out to reveal the things that God wants to expose for healing. Exposure that criticizes or humiliates is never the way of the

Spirit. Your human spirit through direct revelation from God, or a manifestation of a word of knowledge through another believer, are the ways that God will reveal these secrets of the heart. Your human spirit, which Scripture calls the candle of the Lord, can search these deep areas of your heart by praying in the Spirit, wherein you speak mysteries.

In Ezekiel 8, The Holy Spirit is speaking to His prophet and uses unique terms that relate to this specific message and learning about the subconscious. The Lord told Ezekiel to look and see that certain men were performing abominations "in the chambers of his imagery." This word translated "chambers" is the same Hebrew word found in Proverbs 26:22, which is translated "innermost." Imagery can speak to the imagination of a person. According to these verses, these men were doing evil in the innermost part of their imagination, meanwhile believing that the Lord would not see. In Ezekiel 14, a different wording is used, and the Lord speaks that these men had set up idols in their heart. On the outside, for all to see, they looked spiritual and were inquiring of the prophet of God. Inwardly, they were doing abominations. Their innermost imagination and thoughts were corrupt.

I believe the subconscious to be what the Word calls the secret heart, or the secrets of the heart. It is an area that is associated with the soul and the spirit and is difficult to navigate and understand. Therefore, the believer needs the discernment of the Word to rightly judge it and the exposing light of the Spirit to prove it. Hebrews 4:13 makes it clear that we cannot hide anything from God, even this dark realm.

The Principle of Representation

Another principle of the inner healing message is something that I call the principle of representation. Simply stated, this principle says that people of importance or leadership within our lives, especially as children, can affect our mental view of who God is and His character, either for good or bad. The first mention of the principle of representation is in Genesis 1:26. When God spoke of the creation of humanity, He declared that he would do so in the image of God, or as a representative figure. In giving Adam and Eve complete dominion over all other created beings, God was creating them to be a representation of Himself to all other created beings. Adam had the breath and life of God in his nostrils, was given authority to reign over the earth and was initially clothed with the glory of God. Created to rule and reign, Adam was to represent God to the physical creation. Although we fell from this place of stature, this specific calling did not cease, and it has not ceased in our world today. Romans 11:29 declares that the gifts and callings of God are irrevocable. Adam fell, but the law and principle of representation did not go away. For our study, we can see this principle playing out in relationships to parents, elder relatives, teachers – anyone with right authority over us in this way. The principles of inner healing seek to give the last Adam His rightful place as the pure demonstration of who God is.

Although all of humanity was created for this purpose, certain groups within this whole of humanity have distinction concerning this principle. The first group is the individual Christian believer. More than any other, the individual believer carries the role of representative within them wherever they go. Their level of commitment or lack of commitment to the Lord has no bearing on the watchful eyes of the unbeliever who is looking at their life for the fruit of redemption. The Scripture that speaks to this is 2 Corinthians 5:20: "So we are Christ's ambassadors, God making His appeal as it were through us. We, as Christ's personal representatives, beg you for His sake to lay hold of the divine favor now offered you and be reconciled to God" (Amplified Bible). Any act of witnessing is an expression of the principle of representation. As ambassadors of the nation and government of God, we share to the enemies of God that He has offered favor and reconciliation to them. Peter wrote to believers that they should speak the Word of God boldly, speaking on His behalf. (1 Peter 4:11). God spoke to Moses concerning his relationship to Aaron: "He shall speak for you to the people, acting as a mouthpiece for you, and you shall be as God to him" (Exodus 4:16, KJV). God also spoke to Moses about his interaction with Pharaoh: "The Lord said to Moses, Behold, I will make you as God to Pharaoh" (Exodus 7:1, KJV). The cursing unbeliever will suddenly become aware of their mouth in the presence of a bold believer and will mitigate their words because of the principle of representation.

Despite all the positive effects of the church representing Jesus and His kingdom, we need to also look at the potential negative side of this as well. In any cult group that is in rebellion to the mandate of God, you will always find those who claimed to be hurt or disillusioned from their experiences within the church. Those who are supposed to glorify God perform deeds that instead bring ridicule and mockery to His purposes. Paul spoke of this very thing in Romans 2:24. He also had to speak into a situation in 1 Corinthians 5 where a church person was committing acts that were not even named among the heathen. The effect is that the name of God is blasphemed among the unbelieving world system because of the hypocrisy of His people. This is true because of the principle of representation and its concepts. God's people are to speak and act on His behalf, but as in many other ways, actions speak louder than words. Although the unbeliever will not be able to use the hypocrisy of the church as an excuse for their own unbelief on judgment day, in this life, the enemy uses it to pervert the image of God. Nathan the prophet told King David the very same message that Paul spoke in Romans 2. The end of the confrontation to David was that, although God had forgiven him, his deed gave great opportunity to the enemies of the Lord to blaspheme (2 Samuel 12:14). Hypocrites of today can be forgiven, but oh what great place and occasion they give to the enemy and the world system to falsely represent the nature of God, when the Word admonishes us to give no place to the enemy (Ephesians 4:27).

But the principle of representation carries on further than the people of God. Another group that carries this responsibility is the governmental and judicial systems. This was shown in the kingdom of Israel and Judah because of the involvement of God within the structure of the nation itself, but I believe that the concept can still carry through into our day of republics and democratic systems. In Psalms 82:1 and 6, God speaks to the judges of any people: "God stands in the assembly of the representatives of God; in the midst of the magistrates or judges He gives judgment as among the gods. I said, you are gods since you judge on My behalf, as My representatives; indeed, all of you are children of the Most High" (Amplified Bible). As Romans 13 tells us, any authority to pronounce judgment, execute justice, and rule in governmental power, is an authority given by God. This does not mean that every specific person in leadership is chosen by God, that idea is crazy. It means that the authority structure and the concepts of authority ultimately come from God Himself. In Romans 13, Paul calls the governmental authorities the minister or servant of God. As the executer of punishment upon the civil evildoer, the authority structure of government represents God to us as the one who executes justice and demands restitution for true victims. In the Old Testament, the king held much of this responsibility to themselves and therefore was a personal representative of God to the people. This is demonstrated in 1 Chronicles 29:20: "And all the assembly blessed the Lord, the God of their fathers, and bowed down and did obeisance to the Lord and to the king as His earthly representative" (Amplified Bible). In bowing to the king and submitting to his authority as a leader, the people were worshiping God because of the principle of representation. In Isaiah 55:4, the Word speaks of David and his covenant as a witness to the people or as a representative of the Messiah. God is pleased when the government seeks the good of the people and seeks justice and the rights of their people.

Things that we see in nature or in the physical creation are another group that represent God's attributes. In Acts 14:17, it declares: "Nevertheless, He left not Himself without witness, in that He did good, and gave us rain from heaven, and fruitful seasons, filling our hearts with food and gladness" (KJV). The word "witness" is another expression of the principle of representation. We read of this same demonstration of the character of God in Matthew 5:45, showing that all creation received goodness from the hand of God in sunshine and rain, whether they are good or evil. Psalms 19:1 says that the heavens and the earth show forth the glory and workmanship of God. Psalms 97:6 says that the heavens declare His righteousness. Psalms 98:2 says that God has openly revealed His righteousness in the sight of the heathen. Creation is without excuse concerning the Godhead (Romans 1:20). He has given significant witness and representation concerning Himself in nature.

The Old Testament is full of types and shadows, hence, representations of spiritual truth and principles. The three dimensions of the temple- outer court, inner court, holy of holies- are symbolic of the triune nature of humans. Hebrews 9:5 speaks of the representations of the cherubim; physical symbols of what is spiritually at the throne of God. The lives of Abraham, Isaac and Jacob bring out parallel truths that can teach believers about their covenant with God. The event of Abraham willing to sacrifice Isaac is one of the most demonstrative of these truths. We have angels that I believe represent us before the Father, always beholding His face (Matthew 18:10). In the Amplified version of John 14:26, it says that the Father sent the Holy Spirit to represent Jesus to us, acting on His behalf. Any time that prayer is spoken in the name of Jesus, we are speaking of how we are the representative of Jesus, doing on His behalf what He would be doing if He were physically here.

The last group for discussion is the most important for the study. It is a group that God believes in and desires to see grow in strength and influence as a building block of society. The family structure is important for children to be a place of encouragement, a place of good counsel, a place of love. Our earthly fathers are to represent the character and attributes of God to us, especially concerning the areas of discipline, strength, and protection from harm. Mothers represent the attributes of God in the areas of concern, taking care of needs, and compassion. Parents have the tremendous task of representing God to their children, and then to each other. Ephesians 6:1 in the Amplified Bible speaks directly of the representation of parents to children. God designed the principle of representation to operate for good, before the perversion of sin and fallen humanity began to mar the image.

All of us have certainly fallen short of the glory of God in this area of representation of the Father. All of creation, including ourselves, are inwardly groaning because of our current situation. When we as believers begin to grow in the demonstration of 1 John 4:17, a fearless love that carries boldness, a revelation knowledge that "as He is, so are we in the world", we will begin to take our responsibility of representation more seriously. Because of our brokenness, Jesus came to show us the Father. Hebrews 1:3 declares that "He (Jesus) is the sole expression of the glory of God, the Light-being, the out-raying or radiance of the Divine, and He is the imprint and very image of God's nature" (Amplified Bible). If you have seen Jesus, you have seen the Father.

Therefore, Jesus Christ is the only one we should look to when the other representatives of God misrepresent Him. Through prayer ministry, Jesus can show Himself to be El Shaddai, the all-sufficient One. By this, we are not condemning those who have fallen short towards us, but we are allowing Jesus to fill that void in our lives that can be caused by mere limitations of the flesh. People can only be in one place at a time, therefore the busy life consisting of husband, father, provider, mother, wife, child – leaves room and opportunity to accommodate less than 100 percent of the needs of each role. Jesus knew this limitation while on earth as a man; the tiredness, the needs of the physical body, the inability to do everything. He even remarked that it would be more beneficial for Him to leave as the physical person, and the Holy Spirit to come. Now, in the Spirit, He can minister to anyone who asks. His flesh and bone glorified body is seated at the right hand of the Father, but through His Spirit, He is everywhere.

As a means of showing the principle of representation, God has revealed Himself in numerous ways in Scripture. He is Father God, Jesus is our husband, our master, a brother, a friend, and even gave Himself motherly attributes on some occasions. I believe that all these roles, and many others, are in turn to represent a characteristic of God to us. I believe that the critics of the principle of representation and how it relates to inner healing are mostly doing so in the realm of self-preservation and their knowledge of their potential lack in these areas. The revelation of the principle of representation should lead us to intercession and repentance for those we may have wounded, not a self-preserving prideful attitude that always resists the work of the Spirit. Nobody meets the standard, everyone misses the mark, which is why we need Jesus. "He is the exact likeness of the unseen God, the visible representation of the invisible" (Colossians 1:15, KJV).

יִרְמְיָהוּ

III

Jeremiah – Inner Healing Prophet

IN A TOPICAL STUDY, CERTAIN PHRASES SEEM TO POP UP AS IMPORTANT to the revelation being studied or their redundancy highlights a specific truth. In the case of inner healing, the phrase is "God will arise." David used it significantly in the Psalms, and Malachi declared it in his prophecy, speaking of the action of the Sun of righteousness. The prophet Jeremiah is another who is linked to this phrase in a significant way.

Jeremiah's call is one that gives a glimpse into the eternal working of God, His foreknowledge, and His involvement in our personal existence before we were born. In Jeremiah 1:5 God declared: "Before I formed thee in the belly, I knew thee; and before thou camest forth out of the womb I sanctified thee, and I ordained thee a prophet unto the nations" (KJV). This foreknowing aspect of God is a product of His eternal nature. In Psalms 90:2 it says: "From everlasting to everlasting, Thou art God" (KJV). Because of this principle of Jesus being the Alpha and Omega, the beginning, and the end, it seems likely that He would want to minister and repair His people from things hindering their purpose in the kingdom, regardless of where in their timeline these things occurred.

Another concept that Jeremiah prophesies about is something

that could be labeled engraved iniquity. In Jeremiah 2:22 the Lord declares: "For though thou wash thee with nitre, and take thee much soap, thine iniquity is marked before me, saith the Lord God" (KJV). This marking implies a permanent, carved out or engraved significance. Iniquity always implies more than a single or random act of sin; instead, it speaks to a lifestyle, a mindset, a culture of wrongdoing within a person or a family or group. Jeremiah 17:1 also speaks on the deep level of these sins: "the sin of Judah is written with a pen of iron, with the point of a diamond; it is graven upon the table of their heart, and upon the horn of your altars" (KJV). Iron can be related to demonic activity, as the Scripture in Revelation 9:9 describes the tormenting creatures with breastplates of iron. As a strong and sharp edge stone, the razor-like point of a diamond would leave a wound that could maintain a permanent and lasting scar within a person. A few verses later in Jeremiah 17, the Lord declares His work to come against these scars as He searches the heart and tries the reins.

Something being engraved on the heart is not only a negative or dark principle. In 2 Corinthians 3, the apostle Paul told the people that they were epistles written in his heart, written with the Spirit of God. If the Spirit of God can engrave His words upon the heart of His people, then it seems reasonable that the enemy will try and counterfeit this with his own agenda. Iniquity implies a weakness or a propensity toward specific sin in a person and the enemy will put pressure on these areas of iniquity that have not been overcome to engrave his mark a little deeper in the mind. According to the Word, the same finger of God that engraves the epistles in the heart will also cast out demons (Luke 11:20).

As I meditated for days over the principles spoken of by the prophet Jeremiah, I was amazed about the correlation of his message and many inner healing concepts. During this time, I had been doing study into Biblical names and their interesting prophetic insight into people's lives. Because of this timing of study in Jeremiah, I heard the Holy Spirit encourage me to look up the definition of Jeremiah's name. The Hebrew for Jeremiah is *Yah will rise*, which is similar wording and translation to Malachi's prophecy about healing in the wings of the Sun of righteousness. Jeremiah was set apart for a particular message from God and his name gives insight to those purposes. In Jeremiah 4, Jeremiah speaks of an enfolding vision where he sees the destruction of his land and his people because of their disobedience to the Lord. He sees the land desolate and compares it to the time before the moving of the Spirit of God in creation. Although he seems to be seeing a future vision, the images he is seeing are also of a distant past event where the heavens had no light. When our hearts are dark and desolate and we can only see through the lens of past events, it can take the moving of the Spirit of God to instill order and speak light into our being. Jeremiah was shown a past event by the Spirit of God for him to understand the judgment that was coming. In this dispensation of grace, we as believers can be shown these past events in our lives to repent and ask for His mercy on these areas of our being so that we can avoid judgment upon these areas of weakness.

IV

Why Specific Ministry is Needed

ONE NIGHT AFTER A PRAYER/CARE MEETING, MY PRAYER PARTNER AND I were talking about things that had happened in our lives during the previous couple of weeks when we had not seen each other or had a chance to chat. He mentioned that a man in the church was discussing with him as to why someone in need of emotional healing could not just have hands laid on them and believe and receive their healing through those means, like physical healing. He repeated to me the couple of different things that he had said to answer the question; pointedly, that a person pushed down painful events and these wounds are mostly hidden and may need the discernment and love of a fellow believer to help them. The potential for spiritual warfare in these prayers also seem to highlight the wisdom of having other believers around.

On the way home that night, though, I continued to ponder that specific question. Although I knew the ministry to be true, I wanted to find a Scripture that would precisely answer the question for me. Sometime after that, the Holy Spirit guided me to one Scripture. Proverbs 18:14 says, "the strong spirit of a man sustains him in bodily pain or trouble, but a weak and broken spirit who can raise up or bear?" (Amplified Bible). As I began to process this verse, an interesting concept came forth to me. Because our born-again spirit knows the Word of God and believes that Jesus bore our sicknesses in His body, thereby, we were healed by His bruises. Therefore, we sustain or withstand through a physical sickness or infirmity, because we stand on the Word of God and receive healing. Yet, the verse goes on to ask, "but a broken spirit, who can bear or lift it up?" This seems to imply that a wounded spirit can be more difficult to bring to life and restoration and can have both physical and spiritual influence on the person. The book of Proverbs is full of verses that speak of a wounded spirit affecting the body through disease or pain. A child's spirit and heart will go in the direction that it has been shown, even if that direction is deceptive. But, through prayer, the spirit that was taught fear, rejection, and hatred can receive faith, love, and fellowship. A strong spirit that can easily receive from the Lord is a by-product or fruit of ministry that comes by removing hindrances that limit our faith toward God. From my own experience, this faith walk is easier after receiving prayer help and ministry. Before, He was there, but seemed distant and too far away to have intimate relationship. There was a demonic barrier between me and Him. My wounded spirit, with arrows of rejection in it, would not receive His intimate presence. But, as I saw Jesus, filling voids and healing memories, my heart responded and received His love and care.

Another Scripture that I believe shows the need for specific ministry is the parable that Jesus told in Matthew 18:23–25. It speaks of a man who had received mercy from the king, was forgiven his debt, but turned right around and threatened punishment for someone who owed him. In verse thirty-four, it says, "and his lord was wroth, and delivered him to the tormentors" (KJV). Because of his acts of no compassion and no forgiveness, God allowed tormentors to pursue him. This is a picture of the born-again believer who has received the mercy of the King of kings but will not allow it to continue toward those who owe them. Walking in unforgiveness allows demons to pursue and afflict us. Sometimes people are living this principle out because they harbor unforgiveness in the secret place of their heart and may not be consciously aware of it. The tormentors hinder their prayers. In verse thirty-five, Jesus pointed out the importance of forgiving from our hearts. I believe this to include forgiveness from the mind, forgiveness from the will, and forgiveness from the emotions. You can reason out and want to forgive, but if we do not forgive from our emotions, we will continue to allow those wounds to influence us through the emotional ties to those people. Just because someone utters, yes, I forgive you, does not necessarily mean that it came from all the realms of the heart and soul. Just like the spirit is saved but the soul remains unrenewed, so we can potentially forgive in our spirit but carry resentment in our soul. Heartfelt forgiveness has corresponding action that follows it. This principle is brought out in Matthew 6:15: "But if you do not forgive others their trespasses, their reckless and willful sins, leaving them, letting them go, and giving up resentment, neither will your Father forgive you your trespasses" (Amplified Bible). This type of forgiveness cannot be achieved without the help of the Lord. Leviticus 19:17 and the prophet Jeremiah also spoke about hating or imagining evil against another in your heart. The root of bitterness can be difficult to see without the working of the Spirit to graciously dig up and uproot these areas in our lives.

After receiving counsel of the Spirit, we may be able to easily receive what we need on our own. Depending on our condition and level of faith, we should not be afraid to acknowledge that we are not as much of a dynamo as we may hope we are. Better and permanent results are more likely obtained through specific prayer ministry and the aid of a prayer partner (Galatians 6:1-2). Also, Paul said in 2 Corinthians 13:1, "in the mouth of two or three witnesses shall every word be established" (KJV). The Greek word for "word" in that verse is *rhema*, specifying a spoken word. Take the things that you believe God has revealed to you and allow that word to stand up to the discretion and discernment of another Spirit-filled believer. Go back to the example of Peter in Matthew 18. One moment he had revelation knowledge from God; yet, later he was challenged by Jesus as speaking the ideas of the enemy. I continue to praise God for the couple that ministered to me. Sometimes I sure missed the essence of what God was saying and doing; meanwhile, their interaction with the Spirit can edify the counselor as they observe the anointing of God and the supernatural manifestations of the Spirit operating in their lives. Although we try to do things on our own, Jesus has a church and a body that has many members to function as a unit as they are dependent on each other.

The theology of the multi-faceted nature of each human being can help us to understand the need of a special ministry to heal hearts and emotions. In simple terms, our soulish realm can be divided into three major parts: the mind, the will, and the emotions. Each one of these areas has certain duties and characteristics of its own. The Word of God teaches that there is a specific dealing of the Spirit of God in each of these areas and bringing them into conformity to the image of Jesus Christ. In dealing with the mind, The Word of God uses the term "renewed" to specify the workings in this area. Both Romans 12:2 and Ephesians 4:23 carry this theme. 2 Corinthians 10:5 also shows this idea in telling us to bring every thought captive to obey Jesus Christ. We are retraining our mind to begin to think like and agree with the Word in every situation. The next part is a very tough area indeed, the human will. There is tremendous soulish power in the operation of the will, as evidenced by the actions said to have been accomplished by "willpower." To deal with this area of the will, the Word tells us that the will needs to be broken. Both Matthew 21:44 and Luke 20:18 share this idea through the same story. This brokenness does not have to come through brutal defeat or flagellation. That is called grinding to powder and occurs within many who refuse to give up their selfish motivations and pride. However, the godly process of brokenness comes after a person decides to give up their own desires and will and voluntary falls on the rock of the Lord Jesus Christ, following His example, saying, "yet not my will, but always Yours be done" (Luke 22:42, Amplified Bible). Like our Lord, we can win this battle over the will through dying to self and fervent prayer. This battle is not actually spiritual warfare because this battle is not with principalities and powers but is a struggle within our own being. The ability to lay down our own desires and do what God the Father desires is a sign of tremendous spiritual maturity and comes through great stress of prayer and submission, as evidenced in the example of Jesus in Gethsemane. For inner healing teaching, we lastly come to the emotions. Emotions are like other things in life and are at their most beneficial place when used in moderation. It is important for us to be able to feel, to love, and to cry for joy; but, if someone is too emotional, this is a sign of emotional immaturity and insecurity. This can be very detrimental to the purpose of God. In the Word of God, it shows that God's method of dealing with this area is to bring healing to them, through the anointing of the Spirit. Healing of the emotions is one part of the complete work of sanctification and the saving of the soul. This healing is expressed in a prophetic word about the Messiah in Isaiah 61:1, "He has sent Me to bind up and heal the brokenhearted" (Amplified Bible). Jesus astounded the religious people of His day and said in Luke 4 that His being there with them was the fulfillment of this prophecy. Jesus came to fulfill the law and the prophets. Another verse that expresses this need of emotional healing is Psalms 147:3, "He heals the brokenhearted and binds up their wounds, curing their pains and their sorrows" (Amplified Bible). This healing is connected to the building up and repairing of Jerusalem.

It is crucial to understand that emotions are not something ungodly just because they are not part of the human spirit. Our triune nature expresses the trinity of God to creation; consequently, the mystery of three distinct persons, yet one. Although the spirit is to be in charge and rule the soul and the body, we cannot disassociate ourselves from these parts of our being. Ephesians 4:30 cautions us to not grieve the Holy Spirit, causing Him grief and breaking His heart. God certainly does have feelings and can laugh and be saddened. Feelings become ungodly when they are out of control and usurp the authority of the spirit.

There is an example in the earthly ministry of Jesus that I believe is an amazingly accurate account of showing the need of specific ministry in dealing with the brokenhearted. It is the story of the father with his son that had a deaf and dumb spirit, found in Mark 9, Luke 9, and Matthew 17. Matthew says that the boy was lunatic, along with his other disabilities. After coming down from transfiguration mountain, Jesus noticed a commotion around His disciples and went to check it out. The disciples had not been able to deliver the boy and the father was losing hope. He was doubting the ability of Jesus as well, as evidenced by his plea, "but if you can do anything, take pity on us and help us" (Mark 9:22, KJV). Jesus responded to that by acknowledging that if there is pure faith involved, that nothing is impossible. Jesus immediately delivered the boy because He was able to operate in pure faith, no reservations, no doubts. He believed every word He spoke would come to pass. We are normally not operating in these levels of faith, but there is more than a faith lesson to learn from this event. In verse twenty-one of Mark 9, Jesus asks the father of the boy an interesting question, "How long has this been happening to him?" The father replies, "from childhood." This is a key. The enemy's stronghold started when he was a little boy. Jesus seems interested in getting to the root of the problem, that initial incident that gave place or a doorway to the enemy. These doorways can be very dark, but the exposing light of Jesus can illuminate our past. Upon coming into a house after delivering the boy, the disciples were questioning their lack of accomplishment with the Lord. When Jesus responds, "Howbeit this kind", although I agree with the concept of it potentially referring to their lack of faith, I am convinced that a greater meaning is that He is admonishing us that this kind of enemy stronghold, the kind of demonic influence that has been operating in a life since childhood, will need specific prayer and fasting to bolster our imperfect faith to see victory. Also, the words "come forth" in verse twenty-nine are not the same Greek phrase as "cast out" in verse twenty-eight and have a complete definition of "the process of coming out, denoting the origin or place where the action proceeded." Although He gives instructions about specific prayer and fasting, what kind of prayer does He mean? He had just provided victory with a deliverance command, so for us it means more than just a spoken word. The answer is found in Luke's account of the event. In Luke

9:42, it says that not only did Jesus rebuke the spirit, but He also healed the boy. In bringing total freedom to those oppressed from childhood events, the healing balm of Jesus is needed to fill those vacant areas of the soul.

V

He Searches the Secrets of the Heart

IN STARTING THIS CHAPTER, I WOULD LIKE TO REMEMBER A SITUATION that could be familiar to many of us. I can remember as a child that I would dirty a shirt, and of course, it was the one that I was specifically told to keep clean. Trying to hide the evidence, I would take the dirty shirt and cover it up with others in the dresser. This method worked until mom decided to straighten up the dressers or clean up the closet. That sweaty shirt had sat there for over a month and now it had defiled most of the other items in the dresser. There was much more work to be done now in cleaning everything that was in the dresser instead of just the one shirt.

In the spiritual world, we see this situation happen through the ministry of inner healing. As intellectual people, we tend to push down into the subconscious soul all those things that caused us pain or rejection, or where we have defiled ourselves. But, like the dirty shirt in the dresser drawer, it only covers up the problem for a while, while doing nothing to solve the problem. After time, these pains start to smell, creating undesirable circumstances. These pains begin to smell up the fine linen, the righteousness of the saints (Revelation 19:8). This happens when people try to adopt their new godly lifestyle without transforming their soul to match the spirit. Trying to patch

31

the old with a new piece only produces more holes and rips (Luke 5:36). You cannot put godly, spiritual things of the new wine into an old bottle, or an unrenewed soul (Luke 5:37). You must transform the soul into a new bottle that is able to preserve the new wine, and then both will be enjoyed. You cannot paint over rusty old metal and expect the shiny, new paint to endure the elements. Some believer's sanctification process is like painting the godly life over their old, rusty personalities. Later, after the storms have come, the new paint has been peeled away, leaving even more rust. The correct way is to grind away all the rust and replace the damaged metal, sanding out all the imperfections and then paint the surface because it has been prepared to receive the coating.

In studying this work of the Holy Spirit of searching and revealing darkness in the hearts of His people, I have found out there are two main ways that He does this. We need to look at these to find out why inner healing prayer is an important work of God in these perilous times.

The first way is called the spirit of judgment and burning, found in Isaiah 4:4. This type of searching is normally not beneficial to the one being exposed, but is many times necessary in order that the move of the Spirit is not quenched. Throughout the Scripture, the Holy Spirit is revealed as a fire, or having the characteristics of fire. I believe that the Holy Spirit Himself is that fire that Paul describes in 1 Corinthians 3:13 that will judge the works of the believers. At this judgment seat, anything that He did not initiate will be burned away. In the same way, the Spirit of judgment and burning both now and in the future will expose the secrets of a person's heart, if the secret is hindering the work of God. An example of this from the Word is found in Acts 5:1–11, the account of Ananias and Sapphira. If the secret root of covetousness and the lying spirit had been allowed to stay among the people, no doubt it would have caused havoc and may have been successful in putting a damper on a great move of God. Peter was in tune with the Spirit and through a word of knowledge the Holy Spirit revealed to him the secret intentions of their hearts, and the plan of the enemy. Often in the Gospels, Jesus operated in the word of knowledge the same way because it says He knew their thoughts, or He responded to questions that people had in their hearts but had not spoken. This certainly was not beneficial to Ananias and Sapphira, but in the spirit of judgment and burning, the exposed person is not necessarily shown grace. Since Peter obeyed the voice of the Lord, the work of God was not quenched and was instead enhanced with a great awe of the believers by the people.

Praise God there is another method that God uses to search the heart. This way is for the person that is diligently seeking Him, desiring to be more like Him. It is found in Isaiah 11:2 and is called the Spirit of counsel (advice) and might (warfare and victory). I believe the ministry of inner healing to be a major part of this revelation. This type of searching of the heart benefits the exposed individual, because the Lord is exposing it as a means of attacking enemy ground, showing us our wrong motives and attitudes, and then giving His counsel or advice in replace of it. True inner healing is not merely counseling, nor is it just deliverance as in an exorcism. Inner healing is counsel because it deals with problems and traumas and is deliverance because many times demonic spirits are encountered because of the evil situations being exposed. Inner healing brings these two together, along with the healing virtue of the Lord Jesus Christ, to both counsel and deliver God's wounded children.

In Daniel 2:22 we see this principle in action. The Word says, "He revealeth the deep and secret things: He knoweth what is in the darkness, and the light dwelleth with Him" (KJV). In verse thirty of the same chapter, we read the purpose of this secret exposing, "that thou mightiest know the thoughts of thy heart" (KJV). God does not desire His children to walk in darkness, whether it is pertaining to His Word, His will, our own lives, or the secret thoughts of our own heart. Ephesians 3:19 says, "and to know the love of Christ, which passeth knowledge, that ye might be filled with all the fulness of God" (KJV). God's desire is to fill our hearts with His fulness, which we have all received, (John 1:16), so that we may exhibit His personality and character to a dying world. In Psalms 77:6 it says, "I commune with mine own heart: and my spirit made diligent search" (KJV). That

Psalm also speaks of the soul refusing to be comforted. Your spirit will search out your heart because the soul will try to hide its faults and problems. As we pray in the Spirit and draw on the anointing of God, the corruption will surface.

There are other Scriptures that verify the Spirit of counsel and might. In Psalms 19:12, it says, "Who can discern his lapses and errors? Clean me from hidden and unconscious faults" (Amplified Bible). Note the use of the term "unconscious," signifying the work of God exposing things of which we are not even aware. Proverbs 20:27 says "the spirit of man is the candle of the Lord, searching all the inward parts of the belly" (KJV). One way we allow our spirit to search is through praying in tongues, because our spirit prays (1 Corinthians 14:14) and speaks mysteries (1 Corinthians 14:2). The spirit will not only search for the good and godly gifts that God has implanted there but will also search for darkness in the soul. Proverbs 20:27 shows that the spirit is not the subconscious but is the candle of God that is used to reveal our inner part, because only a person's spirit truly knows the inner thoughts (1 Corinthians 2:11). Two other verses are Psalms 7:9 and 1 Chronicles 28:9, which speak of God searching the heart of His people for the purpose of delivering them from their enemies.

I believe it important to show that Jesus operated in both the Spirit of judgment and burning and the Spirit of counsel and might during His earthly ministry. The Spirit of judgment and burning is found in John 8:7–9. This is the account of the woman caught in the act of adultery being brought to Jesus. The Spirit of judgment and burning came to the scribes and Pharisees and exposed their own sin and desire to see the lost trampled on. Jesus wrote on the ground for a moment to seek the Holy Spirit as to what to do. The finger of God wrote the law on the ground as that same finger had written the law in stone centuries before, and then spoke from the Spirit of judgment and burning. This brought conviction and humiliation to those who were trying to execute the law of God through their own unrighteous motives. This is a perfect example of God exposing the heart to allow the work of His Spirit to continue. Jesus came to save the world and the adulterers, calling sinners to repentance, thus fulfilling the law that the Pharisees were failing to execute. The Spirit of counsel and might is found in John 4:7–26, the story of Jesus and the Samaritan woman at the well. Jesus, as a prophet, exposed a private area of pain in this woman's life. But this exposure was to be beneficial to her because He proclaimed that He was the Messiah to her and in verse thirty-nine it says that many Samaritans believed on Him because of her testimony of how the Spirit of counsel and might had come to change her life. The same thing can happen in our lives through the inner healing anointing.

In the teaching of the searching of the heart, we see the need of searching out enemy ground that still has roots in our lives as well as the good mysteries of God that He has planted. This is necessary because the things of the enemy, those roots of bitterness, will choke the Word and hinder the promises of God coming into full manifestation. The life of King Saul can be an example of this principle. In relation to his disobedience in not destroying all the Amalekites and all their possessions (1 Samuel 15:3), his kingdom, throne, and authority were taken away from him and given to David. The prophet Samuel likened this rebellion to witchcraft. Saul's inquiring of the witch chapters later was no more than a fruit of this root of rebellion.

Are there things in your heart that hinder the flow of God? It might just be a nagging weakness of the flesh, but it would seem proper to allow the Spirit of God to intercede for you and show you a root cause of that hindrance. The enemy will rarely attack your strong points, but he will instead attack the areas of brokenness. When that happens, we should boldly go to the throne of grace, that same throne of grace that Paul went to when the enemy was attacking a weakness of his (2 Corinthians 12:9). The throne of grace will provide mercy in our time of need. When we go there, we will come out victorious, because Psalms 41:11 says, "By this I know that Thou favourest me, because mine enemy doth not triumph over me" (KJV). Favor is another word for manifested grace. We know when we are truly trusting in the grace of God instead of our flesh because the enemy cannot triumph over us when we stand strong in God's grace. That is what the Lord was telling Paul when He said, "My grace is sufficient for thee." Paul was receiving revelation in abundance and understanding unmatched. Because of these things, the enemy came and attacked a weakness of his and began stirring up strife and false apostles everywhere he went. Although he had tremendous kingdom revelation, in this instance the simple revelation was, "Stand in My grace, it is sufficient to bring victory over your enemy."

A final verse to look at for this principle of searching the heart sums up both methods that are utilized. It says, "For God will bring every work into judgment, with every secret thing, whether it be good, or whether it be evil" (Ecclesiastes 12:14, KJV). Every secret thing will be judged, as Paul admonished in Romans 2:16. Although final judgment is at the end of the age, there can be judgment in this life. Inner healing and the Spirit of counsel and might is a way that God uses to bring certain secret things into judgment, to pass sentence and condemn the wicked and justify the righteous or innocent. Many people want to wait until death before anything spiritual can happen, but I do not believe that is God's agenda. If we allow it, God can bring anything into the open, although many will run in horror at the thought of their true self being exposed.

VI

The Key of the House of David

BY TRUE CLASSIFICATION, THIS CHAPTER AND PRINCIPLE SHOULD BE in the prophecy section, in the beginning of the study, because the revelation is prophetic in nature. But for me, unless the principles of the Spirit of judgment and burning and counsel and might are understood, much of this principle would be blind and lost. I experienced this while the Holy Spirit was teaching this to me. I had read in Isaiah 22:9 about the breaches of the city of David and I knew in my spirit that this had something to do with inner healing, but I did not have enough knowledge to capture it yet. I left it alone, knowing that the Teacher would bring me back there when the time was right.

By Isaiah's own description, chapter twenty-two is a prophecy of revelation. I believe it to be prophetic of a last day move of God within His church. He desires us to fully know His purposes and plans for the church because the church is the channel that the world is supposed to see God. A reason that many in the world cannot believe in a loving, good God is because much of the church has existed entirely in oppression, poverty, and struggle. Yet, Ephesians 2:7 says that God wants "that in the ages to come He might show the exceeding riches of His grace in His kindness toward us through Christ Jesus" (KJV). People around you see the character of God through your life. God's people should be walking in the favor of God and man, like Joseph and Daniel did. As a result of the favor of God consistently working in their life, they became leaders and rulers of heathen lands that were enemies of the Jews. Businesspeople and Christian advocates that are committed to Jesus should be filling up the halls of Congress in America, bringing it back to godly principles. The church of Jesus Christ is living far below the standard of influence that He has provided for them to live.

Verses one and two describe what I believe to be an accurate description of a growing, maturing church. Isaiah describes it as "thou are wholly gone up to the housetops." Yet the question is still being asked, "what aileth thee now?" or in more modern terms, "what is wrong with you now?" Continuing in verse four, God begins to share what His Spirit is going to do within this vibrant group. Verses four through nineteen speak of the Spirit of judgment and burning. Judgment comes to the wicked, both those in the world and those in the church. According to 1 Peter 4:17, judgment will begin at the house of God. Jesus showed this principle at least twice in His earthly ministry by driving out of the temple those who were making it a den of thieves (John 2:15–17, Matthew 21:12–13). The Spirit through Peter showed it as well in the early church with Ananias and Sapphira in Acts 5. But not all the church is corrupt. Faithful churches are full of on-fire believers that are constantly looking for a deeper and more mature walk with the Lord Jesus. Hebrews 11:6 promises these people that He is a rewarder of those that diligently seek Him. Starting in verse twenty of Isaiah 22, this principle comes to life.

Beginning in verse twenty, the prophet begins to speak of a specific set time by using the terminology, "in that day." It was shown earlier in the prophecy section the importance of this terminology because it shows why the understanding of this work has come about in the past century as a restoration to the church of the founding principles. It seems to have been prophesied that way. Therefore, this day of ministry is brought forth by the coming of Eliakim, the servant of God. Definition of names comes into play again, as it did with Jeremiah. Jeremiah's name means God will rise. Eliakim, the name of the servant of God, means God of raising or rising. The two Hebrew root words used are nearly identical in spelling and have similar definitions. The Holy Spirit is making it plain that the Sun of righteousness is rising in these days with healing in His wings; healing for spirit, soul, and body along with the healing of memories that can cause havoc in your being. The Amplified Bible in Malachi 4:2 brings in the idea that this healing will make you leap for joy, like a calf just released from the stall. From personal experience, I have felt this way after a prayer session, full of joy, life, and freedom, like a calf with its first taste of the open field and running room. Jesus in John 10:9 promised this same pasture freedom because of His good Shepherd ministry.

In verse twenty-one, Isaiah speaks a little more distinctly and says that Eliakim will be a father to the inhabitants of Jerusalem and the house of Judah. Psalms 68:5 tells us that God is a father to the fatherless, the bereaved, lonely person. Jesus Christ parallels these descriptions of the servant of God. Hebrews 12:9 advises us to submit ourselves to God and allow Him to be a father to us and enables us to prosper because we have been made partakers of His holiness. Verse twenty-two is the key verse to all of this though. We find out that Isaiah is prophesying about Jesus and a distinct work that He will do for His people. It tells us that upon His shoulder is the key of the house of David. Not only does Jesus have the government of the church on His shoulder, prophesied in Isaiah 9:6 and seen fulfilled in Ephesians 4:15 and Colossians 2:19, but He also has the key of the house of David. There is significant revelation here about His role to us as high priest and king. His kingly duties fulfill the governmental role, but He also abides as high priest in the house of David. This role allows the fulfillment that He will be a father to the inhabitants of Jerusalem because fathers are to serve as both priests and kings – in charge of things pertaining to God and ruling over the house and family (1 Timothy 3:4). This signifies a responsibility, not a dictatorship or control, that only works as the father submits to the ultimate authority of Jesus over him, reaping submission from the others because they are obeying his authority from Jesus.

To help give understanding to what the key of David can signify, it is vital to walk through King David's life as shown by the Holy Ghost in the books of first and second Samuel. These verses and events show inner healing principles that came forth from the circumstances of David's life.

The first occurrence is when God told Samuel to anoint a king to replace Saul. This is recorded in 1 Samuel 16. In verse four the people become aware that Samuel has come with a message from God. Fearful, they ask the prophet if he is coming with a message of peace, the Hebrew word there being the commonly known term "*shalom.*" Parallel this event with the coming of the Spirit of God to expose our secret heart. He either comes for judgment or to proclaim mercy, in the Spirit of judgment and burning or the Spirit of counsel and might. In this instance, this prophetic moment of anointing for a future calling is for peace and mercy. As we see the prophet proclaim that God is looking at the heart in these matters and not the boasting of the flesh or outward appearance, this message is one of peace and restoration and a greater purpose of God's kingdom on the earth. The next occurrence is found in 1 Samuel 25. Samuel has now died, and King David is going out to do the business of his call to be king. He seeks the favor of Nabal, a wealthy but corrupt man. David goes as far as speaking the blessing and prosperity of God upon him and his household; but Nabal wants nothing to do with him. Frustrated by Nabal's reply, David goes about setting up battle plans. But Nabal's wife, Abigail, whom the Word describes as a woman of good understanding finds out about those battle plans and goes to David to try and change his mind. She advises him to stop his plan of vengeance and seeking judgment on his own. She is a type of the Holy Spirit's work in our hearts to get us to change our bitterness and judgment toward others. True healing is difficult without true repentance. This principle is brought out wonderfully in Romans 2:4 of the Amplified Bible: "Are you unmindful or actually ignorant of the fact that God's kindness is intended to lead you to repent, to change your mind and inner man to accept God's will?" In verse thirty-one of I Samuel 25, Abigail counsels that if he went through with his plan of avenging himself, as King Ahab did, instead of allowing God to have the vengeance that belongs to Him anyway, that it would be a stumbling block, an obstacle, an offence of heart to David and his kingdom. Notice that she said that it could hinder him after he became king and all the blessings of God had come upon him. In verse thirty-three, David blesses her advice, her discernment and after Nabal dies from conviction and hardness of heart towards God, she becomes wife to King David. In verse thirty-nine, it says that the wickedness of Nabal was returned upon his own head. Our actions that reflect the hurt and frustration from others actions are key factors in determining if the exposure of our heart is for judgment or peace.

The next event shows us that Jesus has not only put on the royal robes of rule and authority but has also put on the priestly robes of service. This event is recorded in 1 Samuel 30. The Amalekites had come while David and his men were gone somewhere else and had ravished the city of Ziklag and had taken captive all the wives and children. Upon David's arrival everything was totally wiped out. The men with David began to doubt their mission and had thoughts of killing David. To parallel our lives, if we do not follow Jesus wherever He goes, it can give the opportunity to the enemy to come in and ravish the city of our heart. After this destruction, many believers do as David's men did and begin to murmur and complain against their King, saying that it is His fault that all of this happened. But if we follow the Lamb wherever He goes (Revelation 14:4), He promises in John 10:9 and 10 that we will find pasture; that abundant, overcoming life. The enemy can only scatter the sheep when they are out of the Shepherd's hands by their own choice because John 10:28 and 29 assures us that no one is able to pluck us out of the Father's hand.

The answer for King David to resolve these issues is in verse six. Looking to God instead of at the threats and complaining, he becomes encouraged in the Lord. He then puts on the high priest's shoulder piece and asks the Lord if he should go after the enemy that has ravaged his homes and lands. The Lord gives him the green light to pursue and overtake with prophetic utterance that he would not only pursue and overtake but would also recover all that was stolen.

The last event to look at in David's life is found in 2 Samuel 15. It tells of how Absalom, David's son, was not happy with his place of stature and authority in the kingdom. He wanted to sit in the judgment seat, discerning controversies that arose amongst the people, which is a position held mostly by the king. Through a bit of a lie, he got the people to begin coming to him for advice on issues and the Word says that he stole the hearts of the men of Israel. In parallel, the enemy desires a greater place in the kingdom of our heart. He wants you to begin to trust your mental and emotional resources as a means of responding to people and circumstances of life instead of believing God. If he can keep your thoughts on revenge, bitterness and judgment and get you to listen to his way of justice, then he can incrementally steal your heart away from the King.

This concept of judgment concerning the matters of the heart is a key factor behind the key of the house of David. The key of the house of David speaks of access to the judgment seat like Absalom desired: yet Jesus is the only one that has true access and authority. If we sit in judgment of others because of things of the past that have hurt us then we are asking Jesus to give us the key to the judgment seat, that we may pronounce judgment. We are moving God out of His rightful place as judge and taking that seat ourselves. Jesus is the only one who should have access to this seat, according to the Word. This key of David being access to the judgment seat of the heart became even more evident in the kingdom of Solomon who was given an understanding mind and a hearing heart to judge the people of God. There was even a porch built at his house, that there he might judge. (1 Kings 7:7). This judgment seat activity was discerning the secret intentions of the heart. In one case that was recorded, we see that it takes the wisdom of God to perform this task. The case is found in 1 Kings 3:16–28. The wisdom of God exposed the true intentions of the heart of the one woman and gave the blessing to the other one. In the spiritual kingdom of Jesus, I believe that God has set up in His house, the church, a special section, a porch if you will, for Jesus, who has access to the throne of judgment, to judge the people of God and discern the secret intentions of their heart and deal with domestic and social problems in the home. I believe this to be the ministry of inner healing, the manifestation of Jesus having the key of David on His shoulder. There is counsel of the Spirit; therefore, we as believers need not go before the ungodly to solve matters of the heart but should instead go to the least esteemed in the church if that person is gifted to minister and pray in the grace of God (1 Corinthians 6:1 and 4). Although these verses are speaking about natural things and physical judges, the parallel to the spiritual can be easily seen.

The key of David has both social and spiritual concepts to it; both kingly things that pertain to the relationship to others and priestly things that concern the relationship with God. The kingly-social is called the throne of judgment and the priestly-spiritual is called the breastplate of judgment. In Zechariah 6:12 and 13, the prophet says that the Branch, the Messiah, would hold the position of both offices, both king and priest, which will allow Him to build the true temple of the Lord, the heart of humanity. I believe that all this ties in with inner healing- transforming and building the heart that it may be void of all ungodly things, both consciously and subconsciously, that in the end we will reflect the glory of God in our lives. Before exploring further about the throne and breastplate of judgment, realize that you can exchange the words "justice" and "judgment" and remain true to definition. The Amplified Bible does this repeatedly in translation. This shows that it is not necessarily judgment as in wrath but is judgment as in discernment or doing justice for a person who needs vindication. God's judgment is true and righteous. The wrath or judgment of God is not necessarily God beating up on unbelievers but is God allowing the destruction that humanity has sown by living after the flesh to be reaped in certain measure. Another part of God's judgment can be to recompense tribulation to them that trouble the saints (2 Thessalonians 1:6). Until the final judgment day, God's and the believer's warfare is not against flesh and blood but is against the enemy's kingdom. Therefore, part of righteous judgment on God's part is to trouble the devil who is troubling us. That type of theology shows the word "justice" instead of "wrath" in judgment. Jesus and His Word is the judge of everyone- all will be judged, just not in the same way.

By the process of revelation knowledge, let us take this information about the key of David and the throne of judgment and follow the Word of God that will take us back to the prophecy concerning inner healing in Malachi. Through this process, I believe that we will see with greater proof than before that this throne of judgment that both David and Solomon sat on is now filled up by the Lord Jesus and is manifested for our benefit in the ministry of inner healing.

In Psalms 122:5 it says, "For there thrones were set for judgment, the thrones of the house of David" (NASB). This judgment seat, that now only Jesus has the key or access to, is a throne in the house of David. In Proverbs 20, there are two verses that describe what a king on this throne will do. Verse eight says, "A king that sitteth in the throne of judgment scattereth away all evil with his eyes" (KJV). Verse twenty-six says, "A wise king winnows the wicked, and drives the threshing wheel over them" (NASB). Both verses speak of a sifting, like a farmer does with grain. As people who live in a fallen world, you can be assured that there may have been corruptible seed, some bad grain, that has been planted in your mind. As John the Baptist was prophesying concerning the work of the coming Messiah, he said in Matthew 3:10-12, "And the axe is already laid at the root of the trees; every tree therefore that does not bear good fruit is cut down and thrown into the fire. As for me, I baptize you with water for repentance, but He who is coming after me is mightier than I, and I am not fit to remove His sandals; He will baptize you with the Holy Spirit and fire. And His winnowing fork is in His hand, and He will thoroughly clear His threshing floor; and He will gather His wheat into the barn, but He will burn up the chaff with unquenchable fire" (NASB). Again, we see a winnowing or sifting between good grain and bad grain. In looking back at Proverbs 20:8, it says that the king does this with his eyes. In the book of Revelation, Jesus was spoken of as having eyes as a flame of fire, speaking of the consuming, purging fire of the Holy Spirit that John talks about in

Matthew 3:11. Hebrews 12:29 speaks of this as well. The picture that Matthew gives about the fire that burns away evil can now be taken back to Malachi 4:1 where the wicked are again being shown to be consumed by fire, while healing and restoration are brought to those who trust God. Sometimes this fire is expressly seen during ministry, such as the case with a friend of mine. The Lord was dealing with a false, ugly image of God that my friend had implanted in his mind through a traumatic experience. During prayer, he saw this image, almost demonic in appearance. But then, the fire of God came and began to engulf it, destroying it. My friend then heard these words, "our God is a consuming fire" and a new image of his Father was implanted on his heart.

In having the key of David, the Lord Jesus Christ also took the responsibility of high priest, overseeing all things pertaining to God. All the books in the world could not contain all the effects this has on us, but the book of Hebrews does an excellent job of it. I believe that a specific duty that Aaron conducted is symbolic and a type and a shadow of what Jesus is doing today in the inner healing ministry. It is found in Exodus 28. Although we know that David never actually held the office of high priest, a previous paragraph showed how he put on the high priest's shoulder piece to inquire of God about recovering his possessions that had been stolen.

The duty that Aaron was called to do is found in Exodus 28:30. With the breastplate of judgment over his heart, he would enter the holy place, "and Aaron shall bear the judgment (rights, judicial decisions) of the Israelites upon his heart before the Lord continually" (Amplified Bible). As high priest, he was called to take the situations of life and go before God, seeking His justice, which involves the revelation of both the counsel and the will of God for His people. The articles that were used for this were called the Urim and the Thummim. Urim is symbolic of the light of God, a light that penetrates all darkness, exposes all darkness, and gives a pathway through the darkness. Thummim was an article that stood for complete truth and complete understanding. In this regard, we see that Aaron was a type and a shadow of the Lord Jesus, our high priest of good things to come (Hebrews 9:11) who appears in the presence of God for us (Hebrews 9:24) to make intercession for us (Hebrews 7:25). Jesus has come and put on the breastplate of judgment, and for our behalf, carries the rights of His people before the Father, in order that He may, through the light and complete truth of the Spirit, restore those rights that have been violated so that the people of God can receive perfect wisdom of the will of God for their lives. Through the breastplate of judgment, the Lord Jesus can restore to you those child-like rights of innocence and trust that may have been violated by uncaring or unknowing people.

Through studying other mentions of the Urim and Thummim in Scripture, I believe that we can get an even greater understanding of the importance of this breastplate of judgment ministry. The first one is Leviticus 8:8 and 21. This is an account of a burnt offering. In verse eight, it assures us that Aaron wore the breastplate as God had commanded. In verse twenty-one, it says that Moses washed the inwards of the sacrifice. In comparison, I believe that God would have us wash our inwards, our secret heart, before bringing the offering of sacrifice and praise into the house of God. Jesus reiterated this in Matthew 5:23–24, telling us to reconcile our relationship with our brother before offering our gift to God. When we do this and release all the bitterness and envy from our hearts, then our praise will truly be a sweet savor because the baptism of fire has gone in and burnt out any corruption that would hinder the flow of worship from coming out of our hearts.

Another mention of the Urim and Thummim is found with Joshua. In this instance, only the Urim is mentioned. I believe this distinction to be because Joshua was called to lead the people to possess the land. He would need a light for his path to do this more than a complete understanding of what was happening. Faith does not always have to understand what is going on; yet it moves anyway, trusting God to make our understanding fruitful later. In any event, we see him as a type and shadow of the good shepherd, the Lord Jesus. This is found in Numbers 27:21. It says that at Joshua's word the people would go out and come in. In John 10:9, we find the same thing said of Jesus, with the addition of His sheep finding pasture, symbolic of spiritual food, resulting in spiritual growth and maturity. Through Jesus, and the Spirit of counsel and might within Him, we can be brought out of the flock of sheep who wander aimlessly around, always searching for a supply of food, in need of a Shepherd. These are the wilderness people; no direction, no order, no obedience, just walking around the desert, never coming into the full provision that Jesus has made for them. Our rebellion against authority having now been dealt with through prayer, we will assume our spiritual grazing where He puts us, knowing that He will put us where the food is just what we need.

To carry all this Shepherd stuff a little further, the Word of God shares many things that Jesus the Great Shepherd does that relate to inner healing concepts. In Psalms 23, He provides all needs abundantly, leads us to peaceful waters, restores the soul, which would include restoring broken emotions, gives direction for life, comforts us so that even the worst circumstances do not produce fear, and lastly provides a table of blessing for all to see. In Ezekiel, He binds up that which was broken (34:16), causes the evil beasts (demons) to cease out of the land (34:25) and breaks the yoke of the enemy, allowing prosperity to flow to the people (34:27). In Revelation 7:17, He feeds them, leads them to the living fountain of waters, who is the Holy Spirit Himself, and through Him, wipes away all tears from their eyes. In Ecclesiastes 12:11, we see the second part of Isaiah's prophecy of the key of David, Jesus being a nail in a sure place, further explained. It says, "The words of wise men are like goads, and masters of these collections are like well-driven nails; they are given by one Shepherd" (NASB). A goad is a jabbing stick, something that urges you onward toward a particular direction. According to Isaiah 22:23, Jesus is the master of these words, being a nail in a sure place. Through a genuine Shepherding work, this well-driven nail, upon whom the total responsibility of His Father's house is on, takes His position of honor and glory, and through His wisdom and counsel, uses His words to push us onward past those things that would hinder us from reaching our full potential in Him. The Amplified Bible brings in the idea of all this happening in the mind of the human.

Now we need to give purpose to all of this. Revelation knowledge is not just given to sit on and get puffed up but is given to lead us to a purpose, a direction of God. The purpose of seeking the Shepherd's counsel is determined in three words, POSSESS THE LAND! God is calling a Joshua generation to take leadership in the earth as sons of God. Those with the same spirit of faith as Joshua and Caleb and David should be seeking to subdue kingdoms (Hebrews 11:33). As God moves and directs, little by little we will take the land until the enemy is driven completely away (Exodus 23:30).

This vision can also be found in Daniel 2:35. The concept of the throne of judgment is also in this verse, thereby linking inner healing with the vision. "Then was the iron, the clay, the brass, the silver, and the gold, broken to pieces together, and became like the chaff of the summer threshing floor; and the wind carried them away, that no place was found for them; and the stone that smote the image became a great mountain, and filled the whole earth" (KJV). The things listed as broken to pieces stand for anything that is done without the foundation being Jesus Christ. Iron can be symbolic of demonic presence and clay refers to humanity. Daniel 2:43 shows that part of the dream was that the iron and the clay would mix, prophetic of all the demonic things in the world today that are combining and mixing with the seed of humanity. Back in verse thirty-five, all these things, even those with physical value, are crushed because they refuse to submit to the authority of Jesus Christ. Individually, God will also do this to us. According to Luke 20:18, anything not built on the foundational stone of Jesus will be ground to powder, another term describing the activity of the Spirit of judgment and burning. Either way, these things become like chaff from the summer threshing floor, which is exactly what we saw happening in the throne of judgment. The distinction is that in the Spirit of judgment and burning our lives are crushed with these things, reaping destruction from the seeds of rebellion that were sown. In the Spirit of counsel and might, Jesus comes to help us instead because we come to Him humble and broken. Back in verse thirty-five, it says that the wind, the Holy Spirit, carries these away to never be found again. This principle is getting to the root of the problem instead of just cutting off the top of the weed. Now the foundational stone becomes a great mountain and fills the earth, another way of saying, possess the land. We need the light of God, the Urim, to show us these places of enemy activity that we may not be aware of and then minister in faith.

Another example of the Urim and Thummim in the breastplate of judgment is Deuteronomy 33:8–11. This is the blessing, or prophetic utterance that Moses spoke over the tribe of Levi, the priestly tribe. In verse nine, it speaks to relationships between you and your parents, brothers and sisters, children, and any family members who have influence over your life. This influence may not have always been good and godly. Rejection or abuse can cause very destructive soul ties that Zechariah 13 admonished needed a special working of the Spirit to provide ultimate victory. Verse nine of the blessing says that through the counsel of the Urim and Thummim the priesthood would no longer have to have wrong soul ties to these important people that may hinder them from doing the will of God. Revelation 5:10 reminds us that through the redemptive work of the Lamb of God we are all included in the royal priesthood of all believers. Jesus displayed this very thing while on earth. In Matthew 12:46–50, He was right in the middle of a teaching session, when someone informed Him that His mother and brothers wished to speak to Him about something. In response, Jesus implies that the physical relationships should not usurp authority over the spiritual. That does not mean that we neglect or never take care of the situation, we just do not allow it to have the preeminence that only Jesus deserves (Colossians 1:18). A similar situation from the Lord's experience was when He was twelve years old and stayed back in Jerusalem unknowingly to His parents, found in Luke 2:41–52. After locating Him, His mother, with tears in her eyes and a trembling voice, demanded an explanation of His actions. I am not trying to make light of her instinctive reactions; yet the principle becomes clear. Jesus was about doing His Father's business. If we follow emotional ties from people more than the direction of God, these ties are stronger than our desire to follow Him. It is natural but can affect our relationship with the Father. The Scripture that comes to mind is Luke 14:26: "If any man come to me, and hate not his father, and mother, and wife, and children, and brethren, and sisters, yea, and his own life also, he cannot be My disciple" (KJV). The word "hate" does not mean literal hate, but signifies that this person, including our own desires, have greater influence upon our choices and decisions than Jesus does.

Verse nine also deals with the feelings surrounding the death of a loved one, particularly mother or father. After the death, people become distant and cold, both to God and others. Coping with these experiences may need the comfort of the Comforter to bring them out of the pit of despair. The Amplified translation of Hebrews 2:15 says it so well: "and also that He might deliver and completely set free all those who through the haunting fear of death were held in bondage throughout the whole course of their lives." The last part of the prophetic utterance to the tribe of Levi promises that through the working of God on their behalf that those who hate them would not rise again to cause trouble.

Now comes the big question. Concerning this throne of judgment activity, which is fundamental in the house of David, does it happen now or only in heaven? The answer is both. Romans 8:23 tells us that we have now, the first fruits of the Spirit. While waiting for the complete redemption of our body, divine health and healing are the first fruits of the glorified body. I believe the ministry of inner healing to be a partial manifestation of the first fruit work of the judgment seat of Christ, found in 2 Corinthians 5:10 and 1 Corinthians 3:13–15. In both instances, whether now or at the full judgment seat, the spirit of the person is saved, no question, but his works and deeds are judged and given reward according to them. Jeremiah 17:10 links this with the searching of the heart and the testing of the mind. Paul said that God would judge the secrets of men by Jesus Christ (Romans 2:16). In inner healing, God is not exposing forgiven sin, but is exposing motives and intents of the secret heart. It is the mercy of God extended to our bruised hearts, so that we no longer need to be influenced by those wounds because they are healed.

There is Scripture that declares that this work would not only happen at the judgment seat of Christ, but also now in our lives as the Spirit directs. The first one is Revelation 3:7, which to my knowledge is the only other place where the Word shows Jesus having the key of David. If we take each of the messages to the seven churches spoken to as symbolic of different ages in church history, as many teachers do, then we can say that this revelation of Jesus Christ having the key of David, access to the throne of judgment, is seen in the last days, faithful church. Not even John, the writer, saw Jesus this way as He was revealed to him in Revelation 1:12–16. Every description that John used in these verses is used again in the messages to each individual church, except the one in Philadelphia, where he describes the Lord in a way that not even John saw Him revealed. If anything, this shows even more that inner healing was a ministry set forth to come into a greater manifestation at a certain time and is a special revelation of a work of the Spirit. This revelation does come before the return of Jesus found in verse eleven to reward His chosen so we could look at this as a first fruit reward of ours; proactively, the redemption of our soul in memories and emotions while we wait for the redemption of our bodies.

The other Scriptures that relate this searching of the secret heart to today is found in the teachings of the apostle Paul. In 1 Corinthians 4:3, he makes this statement: "But with me it is a very small thing that I should be judged of you, or of man's judgment: yea, I judge not mine own self" (KJV). From the previous verses, we see that he is talking about being faithful and trustworthy with the mysteries of God. The last sentence about not even judging himself can be paralleled with 1 Corinthians 2:15, which says that the spiritual person tries all things, and is judged or put on trial by no one. In verse four, though, he says this: "I am not conscious of anything against myself, and I feel blameless; but I am not vindicated and acquitted before God on that account. It is the Lord Himself who examines me and judges me" (Amplified Bible). Note the use of the word "conscious." The King

James uses the word "know," but both the Greek and the Amplified use the more explicit "conscious." Paul is saying, on the conscious level, he feels blameless, like there is nothing between him and God. He is aware of the subconscious level where true motives and intentions are stored. He was also aware that God examines this area of our lives, and to be completely acquitted before God, this secret area of the heart and soul also must come before examination. Thus, the principle of revealing the heart in its most secret things, by the Spirit of God. You, like Paul, may not have any awareness of the problem, but the Holy Ghost does. He searches the heart and knows the problem areas, because usually He must wade through them to speak to you. To reiterate a key point, God does this searching by means of His candle, our spirit (Proverbs 20:27). Paul spoke of this also in 1 Corinthians 2:11, saying that only the spirit knows the secret things of a person. Unless through a word of knowledge or other Spirit manifestation, no other believer can know these things either. Psychological concepts can be helpful to categorize actions and reveal partial truth, but the working of the Spirit is necessary for this work. If God does not show something to us, we do not see anything. We should rely on the Holy Spirit for information and the witness of the born-anew spirit of the believer to receive accurate knowledge.

Switching to the King James for verse five, Paul admonishes us to wait to begin this activity of judging until the Lord comes. This reference is to the physical return of Jesus, but the word translated "come" in verse five is the same Greek word translated "lighting" in Matthew 3:16, speaking of the infilling of the Holy Spirit upon Jesus. He filled for the purpose of ministry. From this, I believe that Paul would have us to be baptized in the Holy Spirit before too much involvement in this work. This is because without the empowerment of the Spirit we may lack the sensitivity and discernment to minister in this degree. I have heard people give witness to the fact that they become more aware of the continual, ongoing activity in the spirit realm after being filled with the Holy Spirit. Accuracy and sensitivity are two essential characteristics of the Spirit counselor. According to verse five, after this infilling, He will now begin to bring to light the secret things that are now hidden in darkness and disclose and expose motives and purposes of hearts. The last sentence of the verse shows that this will be God's way of reward, as mentioned earlier, like a first fruit reward from the presence of the Lord and times of refreshing. Acts 8:22–24 shows that God does desire to forgive and remove these destructive intentions through prayer ministry, intentions that were causing a water-baptized believer to be in error. It took the discernment of a Spirit-baptized believer to reveal this to him. It became clear that Simon's desire for supernatural power came from his days as a sorcerer. It is not clear from the text whether Simon ever repented of his error, but it is clear the opportunity was given to him to do so. Opportunity is given to all believers now in this time of first fruit judgment seat so that at the full judgment seat of Christ, our works may make it through the fire. Any work done apart from the leading of the Spirit and the order of Jesus Christ will be burned away. Those who will receive praise from God are those who allow this judgment to bring to light their darkness (1 Corinthians 4:5) and who receive the circumcision of the heart (Romans 2:29). Each of these references from Scripture speak of receiving praise or reward from God, not merely from man. Those who do their alms before men, to be seen of them, have no reward from God (Matthew 6:1). But the open reward of God comes to those who do their alms in secret and their only purpose being to glorify God (Matthew 6:4).

In 1 Corinthians 14:24–25, we find a parallel principle to the earlier reference of I Corinthians 4:5. These verses show the Holy Spirit using other people to reveal what He wants done in your heart instead of just direct revelation to you. This may be needed, especially in the initial stages of ministry as it can be difficult to hear Him when He speaks. I Corinthians 14:22 tells us that prophesying is for the believing believer. Prophesying can be to speak under the inspiration of God. This could include giving a word of revelation from God relevant to a given situation as well as preaching under the anointing. 1 Peter 4:11 says it this way: "if any man speak, let him speak as the oracles of God" (KJV), as if God is audibly speaking to people. Paul taught that that this degree or level of prophesying would reprove an unlearned person and that the secrets of his heart would be made manifest to such a degree that they would bow under the anointing of that word and declare that God is in the midst.

The Lord Jesus has the key of David, the key or access to judge the hearts of His people, the key to serve His people as King and access to the throne of judgment. Isaiah 9:6 is a revelation picture of this. It shows His governmental authority upon His shoulder as the mighty God. The key of the house of David is also upon His shoulder. His names in this regard are Wonderful, Counselor, the everlasting Father, the Prince of Peace. Believers should allow Him to be their fighting counselor, showing Himself as the father that was and is always there, while sharing His peace so that they do not rely on the peace that the world gives. Through the work of Jesus within the throne of judgment, our lives can be like David prophesied about Solomon's kingdom; that it would be a kingdom of rest from all his enemies in order that he could build the house of God, which we are as a habitation of God through the Spirit.

To finish out this concept, it is incorrect to limit the revelation of inner healing and access to the throne of judgment as the only valid revelation of Jesus having the key of David. Because of the correlation of verses referenced here, though, it is obvious that it is a main revelation that God wants to portray. To complete this concept of using this authority of the key of David to shut and open so that it cannot be reversed, an interesting verse comes out. In Job 12:13–14 it says, "with Him is wisdom and strength, He hath counsel and understanding. Behold, He breaketh down and it cannot be built again: He shutteth up a man and there can be no opening" (KJV). These verses link together the concepts of shutting and opening with no reversal to the understanding, wisdom, and counsel of God. In fact, the same Hebrew word is used in both Job 12 and Isaiah 22 translated "shut" and it means to close, repair, and enclose. Notice that Job said that this shutting and repairing is done to a human. This key is not only a physical one but is also a spiritual key to the spiritual city of the heart and soul of a person. God desires His dwelling place for His glory to be within His sons and daughters. The prophetic voice of Isaiah 66:1–2 cry out His desire: "Thus saith the Lord, the heaven is my throne, and the earth is my footstool: where is the house that ye will build unto Me? And where is the place of My rest? For all these things hath mine hand made, and all those have been, saith the Lord: but to this will I look, even to him that is poor and of a contrite spirit, and trembleth at My word" (KJV). The first fruit redemption of the soul is available to those who will humble themselves and seek the Lord to wipe away the tears from their eyes so that they can rule and reign in this life.

VII

Speaking Peace and Warfare Counsel

IN THE VARIED WORLD OF CHRISTIAN MINISTRY, THE ACTION OF speaking the Word of God over a situation as a lone weapon of this warfare is common. Being a faith message and Word person myself, I understand and agree with the concepts of having a working knowledge of the Word, knowing of the importance of confessing God's Word over our lives and learning to believe it and to be able to stand on the promises in faith. Planting God's Word in our hearts and lives is vital. Confessing the Word is important and is a powerful weapon against the enemy.

In Jeremiah 6, verses six and seven describe the spiritual condition of some of God's people, as He sees the heart. There is oppression in their heart, there is grief and wounds, anxiety, afflictions, and hurts. Then in verse fourteen, God says, "they have healed also the hurt of My people slightly, saying, peace, peace, when there is no peace" (KJV). In this instance, the Lord wants more than simple confession to produce peace in a wounded heart, much like the individual described in James 2:16 who spoke words of blessing and peace but would not provide what was needed. Ezekiel 13:10 brings out the same idea, "because they have seduced My people, saying, peace, and there was no peace" (KJV). Speaking peace alone many times is not completely sufficient without the corresponding action of receiving deliverance and inner healing prayer to go along with it, just as faith without corresponding action is dead. In Matthew 4, Jesus endured temptation from the enemy with the Word of God, but complete victory and the exit of the enemy came when Jesus said, "get thee hence, Satan." The confession of the Word combined with believing prayer and declarations are an unstoppable combination of victory.

In Psalms 55, David describes in verses twelve through fourteen how a close friend of his had created strife against him. This friend and David had gone to the temple to worship God together and was someone that he had confidence in. They were at peace with each other on the outside, but deceitful and contentious thoughts this person had towards David in the realm of the heart became manifest and had caused a break in their covenant friendship, according to verse twenty. Verse twenty-one explains the issue: "The words of his mouth were smoother than butter, but war was in his heart: his words were softer than oil, yet were they drawn swords" (KJV). David became aware that people could speak pleasant words and smile but have hatred in their hearts. Relatives and family members do it all the time. They get together with family and smile and laugh and then all the way home ridicule and backbite the ones they just hugged and kissed. With God's help, He can reveal to us wounds of rejection and jealousy that may be root causes of these swords of the heart so that we can begin to love our brothers and sisters without hypocrisy, as Romans 12:9 exhorts us.

Another verse that shows the principle of speaking peace when there is no peace is Proverbs 25:20. It says, "as he that taketh away a garment in cold weather, and as vinegar upon nitre, so is he that singeth songs to a heavy heart" (KJV). Although the garment of praise is the answer for the spirit of heaviness, the burdened heart may not be able to be clothed with that garment without the intercession of another, enabling them to free their arms from the burden and put on that garment of praise. It is like telling someone with arms full of groceries to open the door for themselves while you stand there with empty arms refusing to help. They need you to either help carry the load or open the door for them instead of folding your arms and wondering why they will not go inside. Little children need help getting dressed many times before they one day can do it all themselves. Paul said in Romans 12:15, "rejoice with them that rejoice, and weep with them that weep" (KJV). We need to be able to help unburden the pain of another member of the Body, as we ourselves are members, in order that we all may rejoice in the victory. In 1 Corinthians 12:25, it shows that this concern and desire to bear the burdens of others will produce unity and lack of division among the Body because each member will see their dependence on the other parts.

In researching this principle, I do not believe it voids out or disregards the power of God's Word to change us. On the other hand, it is a misrepresentation in taking one piece of the armor and not incorporating the other weapons as well. In specifically dealing with two weapons of Ephesians 6:17, we need to go back to definitions for clarity. The word translated "take" could more accurately be translated "receive," and is the same Greek word as found in James 1:21. It means that something is being offered to us, instead of us grabbing or seizing it. The word translated "word" is *rhema*, signifying a spoken word of revelation. The Holy Spirit is offering to you His sword, not just the written Word, but spoken words of revelation through the LOGOS, words of knowledge from other believers, or yourself praying in the Spirit and allowing Him to speak mysteries. He uses all of these to discern the thoughts and intents of the heart.

King Solomon's life and ministry can compare to the concepts of inner healing. One such instance was having a special place set apart by God to judge the people of God, bringing godly counsel and wisdom into the situations of everyday life. Without surprise, the book of Proverbs, which is full of this wisdom, talks about the concept of counsel within warfare, the Spirit of counsel and might. In Proverbs 20:18, it says, "Purpose and plans are established by counsel; and only with good advice make or carry on war" (Amplified Bible). The wisdom of God through Solomon is exhorting us to only execute this warfare we are engaged in for the full salvation of our souls and against the spiritual forces of darkness with good advice and counsel. Without it, we may see dramatic deliverances and wild manifestations, but the person receiving ministry may struggle to find that deep root that initiated the oppression. Without that knowledge, they may unconsciously give place to the enemy again and give him access into their lives. Two weeks after the wild deliverance they come back with the same issue because the enemy came back through that root that was not dug up and thrown in the fire. These roots and tragedies of life are the enemy seeking to run you away from that very thing that God wants you to accomplish. God is so rich in mercy that He can bring good out of evil, but abuse in childhood keeps people away from the Lord. The abused may be gracious in ministry to others, but they could have just as easily learned that compassion from prayer and seeking the Lord. The rejected are used to minister to the rejected simply because of the principle of Matthew 10:8, "freely you have received, freely give" (KJV) and 2 Corinthians 1:4, bringing the comfort of the Holy Spirit to others because He has comforted us. I perceive these roots and tragedies as the enemy somehow finding out about our calling and then attacking us specifically in that area of life to keep us away from God's purposes. Revelation of God's will does not come through the affliction of the enemy, but instead through the voice of the Holy Spirit. The affliction comes after the fact of the purpose of God is known (Mark 4:17). God can bring good out of any situation, but He does not need evil to occur to bring His purposes to pass. God would have brought Joseph to Egypt without the help of his brothers. Their original intent was to kill him, thereby ending his trip to Egypt abruptly. The plan of God continued only because of the heart of Reuben and Judah for their brother. The enemy had caught sight of God's will because Joseph hastily spoke about his dreams instead of keeping them to himself. Just like in our lives, the enemy goes out to destroy the purpose of God before it ever has a chance to sprout. The enemy made Joseph a slave, God made him prosperous. The enemy caused Potiphar's wife to try and seduce and lie about Joseph, ending with him back in prison. Genesis 39:21

says, "but the Lord." God's part is always mercy, favor, and prosperity. God wanted Joseph to be a ruler in Egypt, and save lives, and would have sent him there another way. God seeks to heal the effects of the enemy's plans so that we can minister to those He would bring to us. God did this for Joseph in the birth of his firstborn, whom he named Manasseh, which means to forget. The provision, grace, and mercy of God caused Joseph to forget, not the actual events that he endured, but the hardship and affliction of them. Because of this work of God, when faced with the situation of helping or hurting those who hurt him, Joseph decided to help and nourish them, which was the original purpose of God in the beginning.

This same scenario that was played out in the life of Joseph is also seen in the crucifixion of the Lord. We can parallel those things to bring this out. God's plan for Joseph was to get him to Egypt in time to allow him to become a ruler through wisdom and counsel so that people would be saved from the famine. God began to show this to Joseph at an early age through dreams. Joseph would have been better off to keep these dreams to himself and allow the leading of the Spirit to bring them into fulfillment. The leaking of information from the mouth of Joseph gave the enemy information that he would not likely have had otherwise and caused even greater divisions and strife within the family. Thus, the enemy tried to destroy the purpose of God by keeping Joseph away from Egypt altogether by killing him early in life and then by keeping him imprisoned and degraded upon his arrival. God continued to work around all these hindrances to bring Joseph to his place of exaltation and authority in the purpose of God. Our Lord's circumstances bring us to a similar end. From an early age, Jesus knew who He was and what His Father had sent Him to do. At age twelve, He was mature enough in the things of God to astound the teachers of His day. But for all that He knew, He humbled Himself and was obedient and subject to His parents. When they came back distraught to find Him in the temple, He could have responded in such a way that would have caused frustration to emanate from them both. Instead, He spoke a word from the Spirit as to His reasoning for being there and then went with them, entrusting the leading of the Spirit to bring Him back to where He wanted to be. Jesus' immediate family did not always understand what He was saying, just like Joseph articulating his dreams, but Jesus left it alone, entrusting the Spirit of God to bring the revelation of who He was to them. Jesus, like Joseph, had those controlled by the enemy try to extinguish His life, thereby circumventing the purpose of God. Herod sought to have Jesus killed as a toddler. God again worked around these hindrances and through dreams guided Joseph, the earthly father of Jesus, to Egypt, to Israel and finally to the town of Nazareth in Galilee. Growing up as a teenager, Jesus knew who He was, but instead of blowing His own horn of identity, He humbly followed the guidance of the Spirit that brought Him to the day of His baptism, when the Father acknowledged Jesus as His beloved Son, in Whom He delighted. Jesus knew God was His Father before the baptism and the dove. He had spoken of Him as such in Luke 2:49, so the voice from heaven seems to not be for Jesus but to give witness and testimony to John (John 1:33–34). Even after this glorious experience, the people still did not recognize Him as the Son of God, but as the son of Joseph (Luke 3:23, 4:22). As in the case of Joseph and his brothers, when Jesus would speak by the Spirit a word that shook the mindset of the people, the evil within them would drive them to desire to push Jesus off a cliff (Luke 4:29). Jesus had just spoken of His anointing to destroy the works of the devil; thus, the enemy retaliated by getting the people to try and kill Jesus prematurely. Jesus had spoken to the people of their spiritual lack and hardness, but instead of softening under the Word of God, they sought to kill the messenger. The enemy came back at other times, at the lake with the sudden storm, having John the Baptist beheaded, and in the mouth of those who falsely accused Jesus of all kinds of erroneous things. Yet, none of these hindrances handicapped Jesus. But the enemy saved his best for last. During the hours at the Garden of Gethsemane and at His trials, Jesus saw not only His disciples forsake and leave Him, but He also had to deal with the rejection and torture of the people. Although the death of Jesus as a sacrifice for sin was God's will, the Word of God Himself showed how the rejection and abuse was the work of the power of darkness. In Luke 22:53, Jesus said to those coming out to capture Him that this was their hour, the power of darkness. Judas, the one who betrayed Him, did so under the possession of Satan. 1 Corinthians 2:8 speaks of the princes of this world crucifying the Lord of glory. Although the death of Jesus was the reason He was sent by the Father, the rejection, betrayal, and abuse were the works of darkness. Although we are to lay down our lives for the brethren, the rejection, betrayal, and abuse that we may encounter in our lives is the work of the enemy to cause us to dwell on ourselves, our feelings, our pain, instead of living to sympathize with others. If Jesus had given in to His desires, His pain, His feelings, He would have gotten up from the place of prayer and walked away from what God was asking Him to do. For that reason, as weak disciples, God desires to heal those times of rejection and betrayal that hinder our lives, subverting the desire of the enemy. Jesus spoke forgiveness over those who had brutally crucified Him, and we will do the same if we allow the Spirit of Christ to come in and heal our rejection. Joseph allowed God to be his avenger. He allowed God to enable him to forget his affliction and hardship, causing him to be fruitful in the land of his affliction. God bringing this fruitfulness was spoken of by David as God preparing a table for us in the presence of our enemies. The exact place that the enemy sought our destruction becomes a fruitful land. Daniel also lived out this concept by saying that God would deliver him from the lion because he was found innocent and blameless before Him (Daniel 6:22). The children of Israel could not stand against their enemies until they took away the accursed thing among them. We will be victorious when we allow the counsel of the Lord to invade the throne of judgment.

The idea of perfecting God's will in your life through counsel of the Lord is found in Proverbs 19:20–21. "Hear counsel, receive instruction, and accept correction, that you may be wise in the time to come. Many plans are in a man's mind, but it is the Lord's purpose for him that will stand" (Amplified Bible). Here we see three separate ways that ministry may come. Counsel involves advising someone, instruction involves having a situation and its effects explained to you, and correction involves the Lord showing us our wrong reactions and intentions. Not every plan or thought that flashed across our mind originates from God. It may come from an attitude of jealousy or envy. Those types of plans will not stand, but as we allow the Lord to heal that root of bitterness or envy, we can change our motives and close in on the purpose of God. "Where there is no counsel, purposes are frustrated, but with many counselors they are accomplished" (Proverbs 15:22, Amplified Bible).

Proverbs 24 speaks as well on this subject of reversing envy by counsel. The first five verses tell us not to be envious of those who may be prospering through wrong ways or who build their houses through violence. In verse six, it says, "for by wise counsel thou shalt make thy war: and in multitude of counselors there is safety" (KJV). Again, we see counsel and warfare linked together. God is exhorting us to do our warfare by counsel, much like Paul said when he wrote that our warfare is not against flesh and blood. The 73rd Psalm is a marvelous picture of defeating envy through counsel. Asaph says in verse three that his problems started when he became envious of the prosperity of the wicked. In verse fifteen, he makes an interesting statement and says that had he expressed his feelings and given in to his emotions, he would have been untrue and offensive, thereby missing the truth that "the wealth of the sinner is laid up for the just" (Proverbs 13:22, KJV). God admonishes us to follow the path of righteousness. "Thou shalt guide me with Thy counsel, and afterward receive me to glory" (Psalms 73:24, KJV).

Another verse from Proverbs, which is Solomon's wisdom, is Proverbs 27:9, "Oil and perfume rejoice the heart: so does the sweetness of a friend's counsel that comes from the heart" (Amplified Bible). In this verse, we see a picture of inner healing, changing a sorrowful heart into a rejoicing heart, through the counsel of a friend. There may be a place for professional counseling in many situations, but there is something special about friends and brothers and sisters depending on each other to seek God with about their lives.

Another Scripture that seems to refute the speak peace only concept is found in Jeremiah. In Jeremiah 6:27, God tells the prophet of another function that he would be required to do. God was setting him among the people as a tower, to know and try their ways and do a refining work and test their metals, which is a type and shadow of the judgment seat of Christ. In verse twenty-nine, God explains to Jeremiah that He was not pleased with the way it was being done, that all the refining was being done in vain, because the wicked were not being plucked away. The Amplified Bible explains the wicked as the dross, the corruption that has been surfaced by the baptism of fire. Instead of surfacing the corruption and getting it out, we allow the coexistence of the old with their new heart, thereby corrupting the pure metal or bursting the bottles, or tearing the new patch (Luke 5:36–37). The Hebrew word translated "plucked away" in verse twenty-nine means to tear off or root out. The Amplified says removed. This is the dilemma of the Pharisee, who cleans the outside of the cup but does not clean the inside (Matthew 23:25). Our refining work needs to have excellent quality assurance.

Proverbs 25:4 is Solomon's version of what Jeremiah is saying. "Take away the dross from the silver, and there shall come forth the material for a vessel for the silversmith to work up" (Amplified Bible). Paul declares the same principle in 2 Timothy 2:20–21. Corrupted metal is of no value as a vessel and needs to be refined to be fit for service. Revelation 3:18–19 is an exciting picture of this principle. "Therefore, I counsel you to purchase from Me gold refined and tested by fire, that you may be truly wealthy, and white clothes to clothe you and to keep the shame of your nudity from being seen, and salve to put on your eyes, that you may see. Those whom I dearly and tenderly love, I tell their faults, and convict and convince and reprove and chasten, I discipline and instruct them. So be enthusiastic and in earnest and burning with zeal and repent, changing your mind and attitude" (Amplified Bible). The dross must be removed to allow the pure to come forth. Speaking peace alone may heal the hurt slightly; yet God wants our reflection of who He is to be pure. God is our peace (Ephesians 2:14), and His presence in prayer can make the difference in our lives.

VIII

Psalms, Proverbs, and Other Miscellaneous Scriptures

THIS CHAPTER WILL ITEMIZE THE NUMEROUS PASSAGES OF SCRIPTURE that point to the varied concepts or principles concerning the inner healing message.

Proverbs 26:22

> The words of a whisperer or a slanderer are like dainty morsels or words of sport to some, but to others are like deadly wounds, and they go down into the innermost parts of the body or of the victim's nature. (Amplified Bible).

This verse is a twin verse to Proverbs 18:8, the only difference being in the depth of translation in the Amplified version. Like so many of these verses, it seems self-explanatory, but for the purpose of clarification an expansion of them to a degree is necessary. In this specific verse, the wisdom of God through Solomon, that same wisdom that was given to reveal the secret heart of a woman from the throne of judgment, is showing the deadly effect that harsh and false words have on our spirits and bodies. It says that this evil influence goes into the deepest part of our being, the secret heart, the subconscious. In our fallen world, evil seeks to counterfeit the godly. The Word of God can penetrate these areas (Hebrews 4:12), therefore, the enemy will seek these same areas to steal, kill and destroy.

Proverbs 15:4, 16:24

> A gentle tongue with its healing power is a tree of life,
> but willful contrariness in it breaks down the spirit.
> Pleasant words are as a honeycomb, sweet to the mind
> and healing to the body. (Amplified Bible).

To counteract the harmful effects of the enemy's words in our soul, these two verses share about words of gentleness and goodness, words that plant the fruit of the Spirit are part of God's arsenal of attack. A cursing tongue will break down the spirit. The enemy has even gotten people to use the name of Jesus Christ, the name that could set them free, to be used in a profane way. It would seem more appropriate to use the name of the enemy or Leviathan in this profane manner- the Amplified version of Job 3:8 even describes cursing as rousing up Leviathan. James 3 has much to say about the cursing tongue and James 3:2 calls the one who totally controls their tongue a perfect man who can control his body and being. With verse eight, it shows that this does not come from our own ability or power but instead from the power of God's Spirit working in our lives. In verse sixteen, James goes on to say that the wisdom coming from the cursing tongue, which has its roots from the jealous, bitter heart is not only earthly, but is also soulish and demonic. Psalms 109:18 links a cursing tongue with a cursed and wounded inner life. The answer to change the effects of these evil words is healing words. The Amplified version that translates to the healing power of gentle words is from the Hebrew word *marpe*. This word is translated "wholesome" in the King James version of Proverbs 15:4. *Marpe* is defined as deliverance, wholesome, yielding and is translated 'health' in Proverbs 12:18, "there is that which speaketh like the piercings of a sword, but the tongue of the wise is health" (KJV), which again brings into thought the delivering power of the words of Jesus over the penetrating, wounding words of the enemy.

Psalms 13:2, Psalms 25:17–19

> How long shall I take counsel in my soul, having sorrow in my heart daily? How long shall mine enemy be exalted over me? The troubles of my heart are enlarged: O bring me out of my distress. Look upon mine affliction and my pain; and forgive all my sins. Consider mine enemies: for they are many; and they hate me with cruel hatred. (KJV).

In both verses, the situation of a sorrowful heart, a troubled heart, and a painful heart are classified by the Psalmist as his enemies that were triumphing over him. These verses imply that mental anguish and unrest, whether blatant in the mental illness patient or blocked away inside the secret heart of a person, is not something to be taken lightly but is to be dealt with under the anointing of God. These verses ascribe these issues as a manifestation of the enemy exalting himself over the people of God. If a child of God is continually under oppression so that there is open evidence of affliction without any victories, the enemy is using their life and situation to glorify himself. To counteract this, God's children should submit themselves to the counsel and delivering power of God that will enable the law of the Spirit of life in Christ Jesus (Romans 8:2) to become operative in their life.

Proverbs 16:2

> All the ways of a man are clean in his own sight, but the Lord weighs the motives. (NASB)

Proverbs 21:2

> Every way of a man is right in his own eyes, but the Lord weighs and tries the heart. (Amplified Bible)

These two verses show a need for a penetrating, exposing light of God to go into the secret heart of a person, because in our own eyes or through the judgment of our own thoughts we are always right in our actions. This truth is also seen in the process of the new birth because without the conviction of the Holy Spirit upon a life, most people will not readily admit their sinful state of existence. It takes a work of God for them to see their need of a Savior, even though they may be in the worst spot in their life. Even so, because of an experience of hurt or abuse, a person may begin to believe that their feelings of hatred and resentment are justified, even in the sight of God. But the Lord weighs the motives and tries the hearts. The definition of "weighs" is like a bulldozer leveling the ground. No sin is justified in the sight of God, even those that we may feel are not totally our fault. To escape having to deal with it, we justify it to ourselves, like the verse declares. Inner healing is not justifying sin based on other people's actions toward us, but seeks to heal the wounds of the soul from hurts and abuse so that the repentance is more than mere words that satisfy the mind but can be true repentance in all areas of the mind, will, reason, emotion, intent, etc. Inner healing sees "the soul that sins, it shall die" (Ezekiel 18:4) and seeks to extend the life of God into those soulish areas where victory is difficult to come by. "I have seen his ways, BUT I will heal him; I will lead him and restore comfort to him and to his mourners" (Isaiah 57:18, NASB).

1 Thessalonians 5:14

Comfort the feebleminded. (KJV)

Isaiah 51:12

I, even I, am He who comforts you. (NASB)

Short verses. Too easy to pass over. These are verses that show the principle from both covenants of the process of comforting the feebleminded, or fainthearted, or those of little soul. Comfort, if any is to be ministered or received, can only come from God. It is my conviction that this includes, but is not limited to, a special work of healing in the heart from the Holy Spirit, Who in many translations is named the Comforter. You comfort the feebleminded by releasing unto them the resurrection life of the Spirit of God, which is expressly brought forth in 2 Corinthians 1:3-5. In verse three Paul describes our God as the God of all comfort. In verse four, he describes the work of God in this way: "who comforts us in all our afflictions so that we may be able to comfort those who are in any affliction with the comfort which we ourselves are comforted by God" (NASB). In verse five, he states that the comfort comes by Jesus Christ, who works through the Comforter, His Spirit. The Holy Spirit comforted Paul: therefore, he ministered that same release to someone else who was troubled.

Psalms 44:20–21

If we have forgotten the name of our God, or stretched out our hands to a strange God; shall not God search this out? For He knoweth the secrets of the heart. (KJV)

Isaiah 43:9 (partial), Isaiah 46:8–9

> Who among them can declare this and proclaim to
> us the former things? Remember this and be assured:
> recall it to mind, you transgressors. Remember the
> former things long past, for I am God, and there is no
> other; I am God, and there is no one like Me. (NASB)

These verses deal with the subject of idolatry and occult activities
that influence our lives. Whether through direct activity of our own
or curses and influence from past generations that has been visited
upon you, the searching out of these things is a vital part of inner
healing to produce freedom. In the passage from Psalms, the Psalmist
shows the principle that God indeed does search out and reveal
darkness from the past that can be found in the secret heart. For the
dangerously curious child or naïve person who just wants to see what
makes the Ouija board work, that minute amount of time, although
forgotten by the person, is remembered by the enemy as a foothold
or inroad to influence that life. Psalms 44 also says that realistically
we do remember it subconsciously, in the secret heart. Little inroads
of the enemy can have lifelong influence and God seems to think it
is important because He makes the effort to search out these things
in our hearts.

The greatest use of searching is around occultism and its influence
from past generations. Exodus 20:5 and Deuteronomy 5:9 both share
this concept that the sin or soulish weakness to sin from our ancestors
is passed down to future generations. Abused children can grow up
to be child abusers, and so the list goes on. It is a vicious cycle that
can only be broken by appropriating the blood of Jesus and His death
for sin on the cross through prayer. In occultism, many times psychic
abilities and familiar spirits are passed down from parent to child,
aunt to niece, or whatever path the enemy can flow through. This can
occur unhindered through generations to the extent that the receiver
may not even have knowledge of exactly what they possess or the
root of it. They do not even want it. In the case of something passed

down three or four generations, knowledge from a family genealogy or the searching of the Spirit of God may be the only resources for information available. The healing of the soul is vital in this because we get involved in the supernatural during emotionally trying times and if the gaps in our emotions are not sealed up by the Spirit of God, the enemy and seven of his friends may come back to try and move back in.

In the verse from Isaiah 46, Almighty God exhorts all to remember certain things about the past. In the context of that chapter and proceeding verses, He is referring to idolatry. God desires us to remember this so that specific repentance and renunciation can be declared. Unless the ties and idolatrous acts are specifically renounced, the curse may remain as a foothold of influence and the flow of blessing from God can be hindered.

These verses also highlight that our actions can affect hundreds of people that we can influence the greatest. Disease is even part of the cycle of generational sin. That does not mean that the enemy has free reign over everything within a family group, but God exhorts us to give no place to the enemy.

Psalms 41:4, Psalms 30:2–3

> I said, Lord, be merciful unto me: heal my soul; for
> I have sinned against Thee. O Lord my God, I cried
> unto Thee, and Thou hast healed me. O Lord, Thou
> hast brought my soul up from the grave. (KJV)

These two verses are an Old Testament duo that correlate the words healing with the soul in the same context. The verse from Psalm 41 is sharing the need for God to mend by stitching, to heal his soul from the effects of sin. Sin not only darkens the soul, but it can also wound it. In Psalms 30, although it is not the same Hebrew word, in definition the word "healed" is close to the word "bindeth" in Psalms

147:3, meaning to make whole, either by stitching or by wrapping together pieces that were apart.

Luke 6:18

> Even those who were disturbed and troubled with unclean spirits, and they were being healed also. (Amplified Bible)

Hebrews 12:13

> And make straight paths for your feet, so that the limb which is lame may not be put out of joint, but rather be healed. (NASB)

James 5:16

> Confess your faults one to another, and pray for one another, that you may be healed. The effectual fervent prayer of a righteous man availeth much. (KJV)

Galatians 6:1–2

> Brethren, if a man be overtaken in a fault, ye which are spiritual, restore such an one in the spirit of meekness; considering thyself, lest thou also be tempted. Bear ye one another's burdens, and so fulfil the law of Christ. (KJV)

These four verses are the New Testament basis for the healing of the soul. In the verse from Luke, as with others in the Gospels, it carries the concept of being healed from evil spirits or the effects and influences of their activity in your life. This not only applies to physical problems but also mental problems and behavioral problems that have the activity of demons as their root. The word "disturbed" is used in the Amplified translation and it is fitting that sometimes people with severe mental problems are labeled disturbed. They are disturbed in their mind and emotions by demonic powers; in many situations the activity of healing is shown as necessary, which denotes the restoration aspect within the deliverance ministry. After the evil spirits are cast out, the heart must be filled with the Spirit of God and the broken emotions must be healed.

In Hebrews 12:13, this same idea is brought out. Broken parts, or lame parts, need healing. As the limb is an extension of the body, if a limb of your personality (trust, love, hope) has been injured, instead of not caring for it and allowing it to stay out of joint, we should seek its healing so that we can walk in the straight paths of righteousness (Psalms 23:5). Although this verse can involve physical healing as well, I am inclined to believe that the major emphasis is spiritual healing.

The verses from James and Galatians can and should be linked together. Both speak about things in the inner heart that are creating problems and dealing with them through the intercession of another believer in healing prayer. We bear another's burden in intercession. Both verses use the word "fault" to describe the issues. Although controversy has been made over which Greek word was used in the oldest manuscripts, it is the same English word in both verses and can be defined as an "unintentional error." People who explode at the drop of a hat and do not really know why. It seems unintentional on the surface, but if we dig deep to the secret intentions of the heart, while enlisting the prayer guidance of another Spirit-filled believer, the healing and restoration the believer needs can be realized. The prayer partner is there to help bear the burden that we are carrying, enabling us to see the situation more clearly, thereby giving us the opportunity to repent about our motives and intentions.

John the Baptist told the Pharisees to bring forth fruit worthy of repentance. True repentance may involve crying and weeping within a humbled heart. The woman in Luke 7:38 was able to wash the feet of Jesus with her tears of repentance and was forgiven of much. Repentance and confession are not a simple exercise of mind; true repentance involves all the faculties of the being. The Word calls it a contrite spirit. In Vine's Expository Dictionary, this is brought out in the explanation of the word "trespass." It reads:

> The reference is to the works of the flesh, and the thought is that of the believer's being found off his guard, the trespass taking advantage of him. Auricular confession to a priest is not in view here or anywhere else in Scripture; the command is comprehensive and speaks either of the acknowledgement of sin where one has wronged another, or of the unburdening of a troubled conscience to a godly brother whose prayers will be efficacious, or of open confession before the church.

My prayer partners almost always laid hands on me while praying. We do not have to bear our heart before the whole church, but we must openly face up to someone who we trust and respect.

Luke 6:18

> And they that were vexed with unclean spirits: and they were healed. (KJV)

Hebrews 12:15

> Looking diligently, lest any man fail of the grace of God: lest any root of bitterness springing up trouble you, and thereby many be defiled. (KJV)

Deuteronomy 29:18

> Lest there should be among you, man or woman, or family, or tribe, whose heart turneth away from the Lord our God, to go and serve the gods of these nations: lest there should be among you a root that beareth gall and wormwood. (KJV)

The verse in Luke is reiterated because of the connection point in these verses with the word "vexed" in Luke 6:18 and the word "trouble" in Hebrews 12:15. Although translated differently, it is the same Greek word in both verses, meaning to crowd in and annoy. Since the word is used in Luke describing the activity of demons, it is appropriate that the troubling in Hebrews from the root of bitterness could also be impacted by demonic activity. In the beginning of the verse, God exhorts us to look diligently, or take the oversight of our lives. The same Greek phrase is used in 1 Peter 5:2, where the apostle Peter exhorts the elders that taking the oversight of the flock is part of their duties as elders and examples. Jesus, in the Garden of Gethsemane, also mentioned this type of spiritual activity, where He admonished His disciples to watch and pray so that the fleshly, carnal nature does not win over the spirit in a time of battle. Although pastors and elders in the Lord do have responsibility to take some oversight over others and will give account to Jesus about their activity in your life (Hebrews 13:17), the Garden of Gethsemane account is proof that each one of us is directly responsible for ourselves, to take the oversight of our own heart and to carefully look at our own behavior and attitudes. In the last part of verse fifteen, it begins to talk about things that may not be easily seen by us, things that are deep within our being. These roots of bitterness are also talked about in the verse from Deuteronomy because both gall and wormwood carry the connotation of bitterness (Matthew 27:34, Revelation 8:1). The Holy Spirit is commanding us to take the oversight and then pray about these things, because if the roots are allowed to spring up into plants, the demonic activity described by the word "trouble" not only affects us, but the Word says that many may be defiled or contaminated. I believe that to include the principles of generational sin discussed in earlier verses but also defilement in the here and now. To fully exterminate these roots, it takes a plowing work of the Spirit to show these underground roots, or a pressure situation or similar circumstance of a painful memory that surfaces true feelings. This is like the pressure that Jesus fought when the battle between spirit and flesh came to war, when it was time to choose between the Father's will and self-preservation. Then, after it is brought to the surface the final part of the process needs to be undertaken, the part of prayer. Inner healing is just specialized prayer. It is prayer that may involve what Jesus termed "tarry ye here." It takes time to work through the maze of self. The soulish nature needs to die to enjoy the power of resurrection. Jesus went away from Gethsemane victorious, because He had settled His heart before the Father, which will lead to resurrection. When the light of God comes to our own heart to begin to expose darkness, at the time it may not seem too wonderful. Watching and praying takes tremendous spiritual energy and patience and may need the messenger of His presence to encourage and strengthen us after the battle (Luke 22:43).

The verse in Deuteronomy is talking about these same roots of bitterness but shows that not only individuals are subject to these influences, but also families and tribes. We can and do affect others in our families and future generations, if we do not bring to the cross, the stopping place of all curses, sickness, and sin, into effect against those generational things that plague many people. Different ethnicities have known things about them that seem prevalent throughout generations, regardless of their current geographic locations. People are also bound by their unholy image of God. Yet, God deals with His children as a Father. "Like as a father pitieth his children, so the Lord pitieth them that fear Him (Psalms 103:13, KJV). By the patient dealings of His Spirit, He transforms us. Instead of a momentary trick to usurp our will and make us mature, like Jesus, we should learn obedience by the things experienced (Hebrews 5:8). The enemy's temptation is promising fulfillment without any effort and since many believers are lazy, they like the idea of a wizard instead of a father. It is appealing to them. God's way of transformation is line upon line, precept upon precept, from glory to glory.

Job 36:7–12

> He withdraws not His eyes from the righteous, (the upright in right standing with God); but He sets them forever with kings upon the throne, and they are exalted. And if they are bound in fetters of adversity and held by cords of affliction, then He shows to them the true character of their deeds, and their transgressions, that they have acted arrogantly (with presumption and self-sufficiency). He also opens their ears to instruction and discipline, and commands that they return from iniquity. If they obey and serve Him, they shall spend their days in prosperity and their years in pleasantness and joy. But if they obey not, they shall perish by the sword (of God's destructive judgments, and they shall die in ignorance of true knowledge). (Amplified Bible)

Isaiah 65:14–16

> Behold, My servants shall shout joyfully with a glad heart, but you shall cry out with a heavy heart, and you shall wail with a broken spirit. And you will leave your name for a curse to My chosen ones, and the Lord God will slay you. But my servants shall be called by another name. Because, he who is blessed in the earth shall be blessed by the God of truth, and he who swears in the earth, shall swear by the God of

truth; because the former troubles are forgotten and
because they are hidden from My sight. (NASB)

These verses show a principle of deliverance that leads to an abundant life, the type of life that God desires for all His children. As expressed in these passages, this deliverance, especially from demonic influence, is for the believer going deeper into the things of the Spirit of God. The words come from Elihu, who was the only one to speak to Job from the wisdom of the spirit. The other "miserable comforters" spoke from rational reasoning, but Elihu's faith was not in the wisdom of years, for he was young, but instead was in the power and wisdom of God. He also claimed to speak on God's behalf. In verse seven, he speaks of those in right standing with God and their place of authority. Verse eight begins the principle of deliverance, the realization that although one may be in right standing with God, they still may have chains and fetters of bondage that need to be dealt with to secure this abundant life. Verses nine and ten give the solution, which is God showing us the true character of our actions, our true feelings, our true intentions. Through repentance, renunciation, and healing, we can be free from these chains. We must also open our ears to the instruction, correction, and reproof of the Word of God, as taught to us by the fivefold ministry of the Body of Christ. The reward of this obedience is an abundant life that has evidence of the overcoming power of God at work in this life. Verse twelve is a description of those who do not go along with God's principle of deliverance, which results in defeat and loss.

In the passage from Isaiah, this same comparison is brought out even further. God's servants, those who Elihu said will obey and serve Him, are seen with joy and a glad heart because they have allowed God to root out all things that would cause sadness in their heart. But Isaiah then expounds as well on those who will not believe the principle, who cry out from the effects of heaviness and a broken spirit. He then explains a concept that reiterates itself several times in the chapter, that these people leave their name for a curse to those who continue their family name, in other words, generational sin. The last part of Isaiah's words correlates with Elihu's proclamation or prosperity and blessing through God and obedience to Him. Like Elihu's discourse of God revealing to the righteous their ungodly attitudes, Isaiah prophesies that the blessing comes because the former troubles are forgotten. Zechariah and others that have been referenced in this study have shown repeatedly that the Word teaches that forgetting can take more than just a decision of the will to disregard thought on something but may also need a work from the Holy Spirit to cleanse from the painful effects of memories.

Psalms 32: 5–6

> I acknowledged my sin to You, and my iniquity I did not hide. I said, I will confess my transgressions to the Lord (continually unfolding the past till all is told), then You instantly forgave me the guilt and iniquity of my sin. Selah, pause and calmly think of that! For this forgiveness let everyone who is godly pray, pray to You in a time when You may be found; surely when the great waters (of trial) overflow, they shall not reach the spirit in him. (Amplified Bible)

This passage, like the previous one from Job, shows the need of the godly people to acknowledge and seek forgiveness of certain things from their past. Verse six declares that everyone who is godly should seek this forgiveness, so the timing seems to be to get righteous first, by accepting the righteousness of Jesus Christ to transfer to you, then seek forgiveness for past, hidden things in a specific opportunity. Acts 19:18 in the Amplified speaks of believers coming and making full confession and thoroughly exposing the deeds of their past. Part of this timing is because if you are not secure in your relationship with the Lord and that you have inherited His righteousness to your account, when the darkness begins to surface, many people would begin to lose security or confidence in their salvation. The last phrase in most translations carries the idea of this opportunity of forgiveness as happening in a time when God can be found. This obviously does fit the circumstance of specific healing prayer as led by the Spirit, but the margin note in my King James Bible says that the literal Hebrew means in a time of finding. This agrees with the other translations, yet it could also include the meaning as a time of finding out, or searching out, a specific time when the Spirit of God helps us to find out and search out our hearts. The reference in the New American Standard says exactly this point. We may be the ones that need to be found out by God.

Psalms 119:26

I have declared my ways and opened my griefs to You, and You listened to me. (Amplified Bible)

Psalms 119:24, 111

Thy testimonies also are my delight and my counselors. Thy testimonies have I taken as a heritage forever; for they are the rejoicing of my heart. (KJV)

John 15:26

But, when the Comforter is come, Whom I will send unto you from the Father, the Spirit of truth, which proceedeth from the Father, He shall testify of Me. (KJV)

These verses show a biblical principle of true Christian counseling. The first verse, from the Amplified Bible, shows the believer opening wide their heart to God, telling of their ways, their course of action, their lifestyle and the things that have caused them grief. God is a patient listener, but He always has a response or an answer to a problem. The word "testimony" is used twice in the verses from Psalms 119 and speaks of the testimony of God to the believer as a counselor that becomes a rejoicing of the heart. In John, Jesus declares that the Spirit would testify, or give testimony about Him. Therefore, through prayer, and through either word or vision, the Holy Spirit will testify to the believer about Jesus, giving testimony for the King of kings about what He was doing during that time of grief in our lives. Obviously that grace, comfort, and presence was not received at the actual event, but the God who lives in eternity, can manifest it again to our wounded heart that it may be received now.

2 Corinthians 4:2

> We have renounced disgraceful ways (secret thoughts, feelings, desires and underhandedness, the methods and acts that men hide through shame). (Amplified Bible)

Psalms 69:20

> Reproach hath broken my heart. (KJV)

Romans 13:12

> Let us therefore cast off the works of darkness, and let us put on the armor of light. (KJV)

1 Corinthians 13:11

> When I was a child, I spake as a child, I understood as a child, I thought as a child: but when I became a man, I put away childish things. (KJV)

John 20:22–23

> And when He had said this, He breathed on them, and
> saith unto them, Receive ye the Holy Ghost: whose
> soever sins ye remit, they are remitted unto them; and
> whose soever sins ye retain, they are retained. (KJV)

These verses all describe an activity that every believer should
eventually be involved in. It seems that the time that it should
happen in a life is (1) because of the ministry of reconciliation
becoming reality, (2) our salvation being nearer than when we first
believed, (3) living in a realm of spiritual growth called adulthood,
and (4) after receiving the fullness of the Spirit. It is the mercy and
grace of God to secure us in His foundation before attempting to
apply pressure and grow us up even further. In the verse from 2
Corinthians, the apostle Paul speaks of a personal renouncing or
disowning of ourselves from secret thoughts, feelings, and hidden
things of shame. The word translated "hidden things" in the King
James of 2 Corinthians 4:2 is the same Greek word that he used in
1 Corinthians 14:25, translated "the secrets of his heart." This is
undoubtedly where the Amplified gets the idea of secret thoughts
and feelings. In relevant terms, the Holy Spirit is admonishing us to
renounce, not just confess, our subconscious thoughts and feelings
that prove to be ungodly. Confession implies that you would agree
that it is wrong but renouncing means that the thoughts will lose
their authority and power and ownership over the believer. The end
of the verse says that these things that we need to renounce are things
of shame, shameful to us, to others and to the Lord. This is where
the verse from Psalms comes in because the definition of the word
translated "reproach" is "disgrace and shame," which connects with
2 Corinthians. The Psalmist described this shame as something
that breaks or wounds the heart. Putting that together, the believer
is to renounce any subconscious attitudes and thoughts that are
ungodly, even if the shame comes from our own heart being broken

by someone else's actions against us. This can be part of the ministry of reconciliation.

In Romans, Paul reiterated this message. He is teaching on love and obedience to others. He is obviously directing his words to the more spiritually mature believers, because in verse eleven he says that their salvation was closer to them then when they first believed. To this group, he exhorts, "cast off the works of darkness." These same works of darkness are found in Ephesians 5:11 and are unfruitful to the cause of Christ, are to be reproved by us and are brought out in the open and made visible by the light of God.

In 1 Corinthians 13, Paul is speaking of a putting away of childish things. Starting in verse eight, the King James uses the words "fail, vanish away, done away and put away" to translate the same Greek word that is used in all those verses. It could be expanded to mean to render useless and made of no effect. So, to paraphrase verse eleven, the believer should render useless and make void the effectiveness of childish things in our lives. Note the timing of this activity as after the realization of adulthood in the spiritual realm. Obviously, God is not limited to this timeframe, but the need for keen discernment, an ear to hear and a desire and will to serve God completely are more readily found in a more mature believer. God wants no evil influence upon us, especially those childish things. The Greek word for childish is *nepios*, meaning no speech, which signifies a baby or toddler. This gives significant reference to the experiences of being in the womb and the first influential years of life.

In John 22, the timing within the spiritual walk is reiterated as it is after the receiving of the Spirit, the same receiving done in Acts 19:2 where they spoke in tongues and prophesied. In verse twenty-three, Jesus declared "whose soever sins ye remit, they are remitted unto them" (KJV). To remit is to forgive, let go, forsake, lay aside, etc. This total forgiveness will need the power and presence of the Spirit of God to see it fully manifest. We can have no confidence in the flesh concerning these matters of heart forgiveness. When true forgiveness occurs, the effect of those sins can be broken, regardless of the circumstance of the others involved. This same principle of letting go or keeping within ourselves the sins of others against us is also found in Matthew 18:15–35. From the beginning of verse fifteen and through the parable to the end of verse thirty-five, the context is forgiveness toward others. So, in verse eighteen, the binding and loosing is talking about the fault of thy brother against you, to either bind it (retain) or to loose it (remit). In the following parable, there is a picture of the forgiven unforgiver, who because of heart unforgiveness, was delivered to the tormentors. Because of the unforgiveness that we conceive in our own heart we are delivered to the enemy of our soul. Through the word of knowledge, Peter asked Ananias in Acts 5:4 why he had conceived the act of rebellion in his heart. The enemy came to fill his heart and give power to the idea, but it was conceived in the human heart. Because the heart, and potentially the secret heart, is where the roots of these sins originate, this is where the forgiveness must come from. These areas would include the thoughts, will, and emotions.

Psalms 7:9

> Oh let the wickedness of the wicked come to an end: but establish the just: for the righteous God trieth the hearts and reins. (KJV)

Psalms 16:7–8

> I will bless the Lord, Who hath given me counsel: my reins will also instruct me in the night seasons. I have set the Lord always before me: because He is at my right hand, I shall not be moved. (KJV)

Psalms 139:23–24

> Search me, O God, and know my heart: try me, and
> know my thoughts: and see if there be any wicked way
> (Hebrew: 'way of pain or grief') in me and lead me in
> the way everlasting. (KJV)

Philippians 3:5

> Let us therefore, as many as be perfect, be thus
> minded: and if in any thing ye be otherwise minded,
> God shall reveal even this unto you. (KJV)

All these verses declare the principle of God establishing and perfecting the believer's life by the trying, searching, and revealing work of the Holy Spirit. In Psalms 7:9, it declares the end of the wicked in our lives and the establishing of God's kingdom of righteousness, peace, and joy in the Holy Ghost within our hearts because a holy and righteous Father searches the hearts and reins (emotions) of His children. In Psalms 16, the counsel of God is praised because it has worked out for the emotions to come into a place of salvation so they can be used by God to instruct His children though dreams. Because of this instruction, the believer is brought to a place of complete surrender to the purpose of God, steadfast and immovable, always abounding in the work of the Lord (1 Corinthians 15:58). In Psalms 139, the Psalmist leads the disciple in a prayer for inner healing. When it is asked of God to know the thoughts and hearts, I am convinced that it is referring to the secret thoughts and heart, because Psalms 139:4 declares, "For there is not a word in my tongue, but lo, O Lord, thou knowest it altogether," (KJV) and Ezekiel 11:5 says, "for I (God) know the things that come into your mind, every one of them" (KJV). Amos 4:13 carries this same idea, "and declareth unto man what is his thought" (KJV). Although it may not be clear if the pronoun "his" refers to God declaring His divine thoughts to humanity instead of God showing us our thoughts, I believe that either one fits the narrative of God revealing secret things to a person. Once this activity is realized, the searching out is for any wicked way or mode of action or lifestyle, or as the margin reference says, "way of pain or grief." The path of righteousness or the way everlasting is replacing or healing those ways of pain and grief with the life of God. Philippians 3:15 is the new covenant verse declaring this principle. The high calling of full maturity and the obtaining of the glory of the Lord Jesus (2 Thessalonians 2:14) should be the desire of every believer. In following this calling, Paul admonished that if in anything, if we have feelings of going backward, of slacking off, of giving up, all things that are otherwise minded and contrary to pressing forward to perfection, that God will reveal this. He does this because God has no pleasure in the one that draws back or falls away (Hebrews 10:38). These things that pull the believer from the prize in Philippians are the same weights and sin that beset the believer in running their race in Hebrews. By looking unto Jesus, the author of faith, we can be with those of Paul's company who do not draw back but believe to the complete saving of the soul, the end of our faith. This is not describing initial salvation but refers to the complete and total restoration of the soul to align with the spirit and the Spirit of God to where it is blameless in every area. Our spirit received it when we were born anew, but Peter declares that the salvation of the soul was the end of our faith. It happens day by day (2 Corinthians 4:16), but there are also times of specific ministry when we, by the revealing light of the Spirit of God, can jump from one plateau to another. Mental reasoning and analyzing can bring some truth but are usually a death struggle – that would be crucifixion without resurrection, ever learning but never able to come to the knowledge of the truth. God's purpose is for resurrection and His power and wisdom can make it happen suddenly. "A scorner seeketh wisdom, and findeth it not: but knowledge is easy unto him that understandeth" (Proverbs 14:6, KJV).

Romans 7:18–19

> For I know that in me (that is, in my flesh), dwelleth
> no good thing: for to will is present with me: but how
> to perform that which is good I find not. For the good
> that I would I do not: but the evil which I would not,
> that I do. (KJV)

James 4:17

> Therefore to him that knoweth to do good, and doeth
> it not, to him it is sin. (KJV)

These two verses show a specific principle of a problem area of the soul. In Romans, Paul establishes the fact that the will or desire to do what is right was present in him. Once born from above, out of love for God and respect for the covenant blood of Jesus, the believer wants to do right; yet, that desire is not always enough to enable the believer to perform that which is right. James declares that it is possible to also have knowledge and understanding of what is good, and still not do it. The will and the mind can be on board to do right, but the part of our personality that can dominate our being and hinder the righteous actions of the believer is the emotions and the sin principle within them that seeks to avenge and justify itself. From the prophecy of Isaiah 61, the Word declares that it takes the anointing of the Spirit to heal the brokenhearted and a calling from God. Emotional weakness, insecurity and mental torment are signals that something inside is not right, like physical pain is a signal of something wrong within the body. The Lord is nigh or near to them that are of a broken heart (Psalms 34:18).

Psalms 56:8

Thou tellest my wanderings: put Thou my tears into Thy bottle: are they not in Thy book? (KJV)

Psalms 139:16

Thine eyes have seen my unformed substance; and in Thy book they were all written, the days that were ordained for me, when as yet there was not one of them. (NASB)

Revelation 7:17

For the Lamb which is in the midst of the throne shall feed them and shall lead them unto living fountains of waters: and God shall wipe away all tears from their eyes. (KJV)

Psalms 116:8

For thou hast delivered my soul from death, mine eyes from tears, and my feet from falling. (KJV)

Revelation 21:4

And God shall wipe away all tears from their eyes: and there shall be no more death, neither sorrow, nor crying, neither shall there be any more pain: for the former things are passed away. (KJV)

All these verses tell of the awesome compassion of our God and His activity surrounding the tears of His people. Let it be known that God is aware of every tear of sorrow that has been wept by His children. He has also made provision for them to be turned into tears of joy. One of the reasons that Jesus had to suffer the rejection of His people, His family, His friends, and eventually Father God, was so that He can now be a high priest that is moved by compassion towards those who have suffered rejection from those that they trusted. In Psalms 56:8, the writer says that God will tell, or declare the wanderings or exiled feelings of someone. This wandering may be to try and find acceptance. The last three verses speak of God wiping away tears from the eyes. Although the full manifestation of this will be in the new heaven, God's promises are for this life as well and we should have the first fruits of the Spirit operating in our lives, thus waiting for the redemption of our body (Romans 8:23). Part of these first fruit blessings are the workings of God for the salvation of the soul. We should strive to walk in the dynamite powers of the age to come when we fully understand the foundation that we are standing on and decide to go on to complete maturity (Hebrews 6:1, 5). In Psalms 116:8, God removed tears of sorrow and suicide, because in verse three the phrase "sorrows of death" can mean a pledge of death, or an inner vow or death wish. It is deep depression that brings a person into a state of wishing they were dead. The compassion of God to interact against this depression is found in Revelation 21:4, which can also be looked at from this first fruit perspective. The language "former things passed away, all things made new" is the same language as the declaration of Paul in 2 Corinthians 5:17, speaking about the new birth in Christ. As a result of being in Christ and knowing Him after the Spirit, the believer can find their tears wiped away and the removal of the sorrow. There can be no more bondage to death because Christ Jesus has abolished death and has brought life and immortality to light (2 Timothy 1:10). The word translated "abolished" there is the same Greek word as in 1 Corinthians 13:8, 10 and 11, and means to be rendered useless and of no effect. Inner healing prayer and knowing Jesus after the Spirit brings your mind and emotions into the flow with the reality of the work of the new birth, as physical healing brings the physical body into that flow until its final redemption of the new body. This may be what Paul meant in saying to "work out your own salvation with fear and trembling" (Philippians 2:12). "Work out" means to "work fully, accomplish, finish, fashion," much like the promise in Philippians 1:6 that Jesus has begun a good work in the believer's life, and He will complete it. The complete redemptive work was accomplished by Jesus on the cross; our lives are to be a continually growing understanding of what He did and what the resurrection accomplished, as our eyes of understanding become increasingly enlightened (Ephesians 1:18). The path of the just is to be exactly that path that becomes brighter and brighter until the appointed day (Proverbs 4:18). Inner healing prayer and ministry are part of that growing light of God that illuminates our path. "Unto the upright there ariseth light in the darkness" (Psalms 112:4, KJV).

Psalms 129:1–4

> Many a time have they afflicted me from my youth.
> May Israel now say: many a time have they afflicted
> me from my youth: yet they have not prevailed against
> me. The plowers plowed upon my back: they have
> made long their furrows. The Lord is righteous: He
> hath cut asunder the cords of the wicked. (KJV)

This passage shares the feelings and mental vocabulary of someone who was consistently abused as a child either through physical, verbal, or sexual abuse. The first statement is a sentence said by the afflicted before the redemptive intervention of God. The second statement is a declaration of victory. God's work will also break the ties that influence the victim long after the abuse is over so that the victory can be seen in a demonstrative way. This same principle is also brought forth in Romans 3:25–26. The Word declares, "Whom" (speaking of Jesus) "God displayed publicly as a propitiation in His blood through faith. This was to demonstrate His righteousness, because in the forbearance of God He passed over the sins previously committed; for the demonstration, I say, of His righteousness at the present time, that He might be just and the justifier of the one who has faith in Jesus" (NASB). God displayed publicly His Son, for all eyes to see, as a mercy seat to exhibit God's righteousness in showing mercy. Even today, through the public display of Jesus, called the demonstration or manifestation of the Spirit through the gifts of healings (1 Corinthians 2:4, 12:7), God is still seeking to display His righteousness and His mercy seat, Who can justify the believer that believes in the work of the cross. This is God's way to counsel and judge, and since the judgment is God's (Deuteronomy 1:17), His judges in the earth should do the same, allowing God to be with us in the matter of judgment (2 Chronicles 19:6). Inner healing can be God bringing righteous judgment within a particular situation, sometimes through vision, by justifying the innocent and the victim of abuse and condemning the wicked or the abuser. Human wisdom and efforts can be lacking in proper compassion or power for this work; therefore, a work of the Spirit is necessary. If the blood of bulls and goats cannot resolve the guilty conscience of the old covenant person, soulish wisdom to justify a victim seems powerless as well. Only by appropriating through prayer the blood of Jesus, the spotless Lamb, can the conscience be purged, and the inner heart renewed, as they see the mercy seat of God at this present time that provides demonstrative victory in a life.

Jeremiah 11:18–20

> Moreover, the Lord made it known to me and I know it; then Thou didst show me their deeds. But I was like a gentle lamb led to the slaughter; and I did not know that they had devised plots against me, saying, "Let us destroy the tree with its fruit, and let us cut him off from the land of the living, that his name be remembered no more." But, O Lord of hosts, Who

judges righteously, Who tries the feelings and the heart, let me see Thy vengeance on them, for to Thee have I committed my cause. (NASB)

Jeremiah 20:12

Yet, O Lord of hosts, Thou Who does test the righteous, Who seest the mind and the heart; let me see Thy vengeance on them; for to Thee I have set forth my cause. (NASB)

Jeremiah 17:10

I, the Lord, search the heart, I test the mind, even to give to each man according to his ways, according to the results of his deeds. (NASB)

Jeremiah 32:19

Great in counsel and mighty in deed, Whose eyes are open to all the ways of the sons of men, giving to everyone according to his ways and according to the fruit of his deeds. (NASB)

The revelation of these verses can be two-fold. All of them, along with references from 2 Corinthians 5:10, Revelation 22:12, Ecclesiastes 12:14 among others, link the searching of the heart, the bringing of the secret heart into judgment, by God, with His reward according to their ways. Ultimately and completely, this will happen at the future judgment seat of Christ, which Solomon was a type and a shadow of in 1 Kings 7:7. The Old Testament dispensation was a shadow of the good things to come (Colossians 2:17, Hebrews 10:1), and there is a first fruit version of this judgment that I believe can be demonstrated through inner healing.

The first verse from Jeremiah 11 is the main text for the other revelation along with Jeremiah 20:12, which is part of an utterance that comes right between two instances of the persecuted prophet in the middle of complaining and murmuring. He even went as far as saying that he wished that he had not been born and cursed the day of his birth, like Job. When God initially spoke to Jeremiah, He spoke to him about His presence with him and guiding him in the womb and his calling before he was born. Jeremiah was like us, as Mark 4:17 teaches, that when affliction or persecution comes because of the Word of God, those without a strong root system can be offended. Persecution or pressure on the soul to preserve itself exposes the true condition of the heart. Jeremiah did not stay in this realm; indeed, he wrote down a solution to the problem of having a cold, stony, hard heart that even though it may receive the word with gladness, cannot endure the time of persecution or pressure.

The first part of the solution is that God will reveal to the believer the actions and plots of the enemy against our lives. Although it could be direct demonic activity, it is more likely to be masqueraded within the lives of others who have strong influence. Jeremiah's words of being a gentle lamb and unaware of the device of the enemy is descriptive of a little child. Ignorance to the devices of the enemy gives him an advantage over us (2 Corinthians 2:11). Without the covering of the parents, especially the father, little children are vulnerable to these plots against them. "Examine me, O Lord, and prove me; try my reins and my heart" (Psalms 26:2, KJV). This is the second part of the solution; the cry for help from the believer. The reward comes as we see the vengeance of God in action. Notice it says "see," implying with the eyes of the spirit first and then experientially in the physical realm. In circumstances of abuse, rejection and grief, God's vengeance is not necessarily a swift hand or wrath towards the abuser. Seeing walls and barriers that the enemy has worked a lifetime in building between people and families being brought down to the ground could be a sign of God's vengeance. Many times, this warfare is not against flesh and blood, but the enemy of our soul. "The righteous shall rejoice when he seeth the vengeance: he shall wash his feet in the blood of the wicked. So that a man shall say, verily there is a reward for the righteous: verily He is a God that judgeth in the earth (Psalms 58:10–11, KJV).

Galatians 2:11

But when Peter was come to Antioch, I withstood him to the face, because he was to be blamed. (KJV)

John 15:22

If I had not come and spoken unto them, they had not had sin; but now they have no cloak for their sin. (KJV)

1 Corinthians 4:3–4

But to me it is a very small thing that I should be examined by you, or by any human court; in fact, I do not even examine myself. I am conscious of nothing against myself, yet I am not by this acquitted; but the One Who examines me is the Lord. (NASB)

The world is full of shallow people. Full-scale commitment and dedication are hard to find. Very few people have a desire to rock the boat or stir up the mire of blackness that the world lives in because it takes effort and a risk of being persecuted. In the church, it can be similar. God wants us to go forward and get deep enough into the river to be where we are taken away by the current and can only swim along with the water (Ezekiel 47:1–5). Ankle-deep people can still rely on their own footing for safety. Water that sweeps you away takes away that self-reliance. To motivate the shallow people, God has placed an anointing in His church called the prophet. When Samuel would walk into a town, all the elders of the city would get scared (1 Samuel 16:4). Although not done arrogantly, Samuel carried the authority of his position in God, and everyone knew it. Elisha knew the words of the enemy king and all his battle plans (2 Kings 6:12). The new covenant has prophets as well. In Malachi 4:5–6, it declares that the prophetic anointing would cause the heart of the fathers to turn to the children and the heart of the children to turn to their fathers. Part of this may involve digging deep into the secret realm of the heart to stop the pronounced judgment of the curse because of broken family relationships.

All three of the verses deal with the concept of meeting face-to-face with our secret intentions and motives. According to Paul, it was not enough to be able to stand justified in the sight of other men or even in the arena of mental awareness where we would examine ourselves with the standards of ethics and morals. Full justification comes after the judgment of God upon the secret heart. It is possible to live the moral, Christian life without having this meeting with the darkness within ourselves, but we take the risk of blocking the light and life of God.

This type of face-to-face confrontation with the secret heart happened in the book of Galatians. Paul confronted a brother with a situation in his heart that was potentially influencing other Jews and Barnabas (Galatians 2:13). In like manner, God can show us the secret nature of our hearts through a vision of specific memories or situations in our past and/or words of knowledge or prophetic utterance from a brother or sister in the Lord (1 Corinthians 14:25). This confrontation will make us come face-to-face with the secrets in our own lives. Without exposure, corrupt roots can use up room where good roots could be growing while also feeding the tree bad nutrients. Jesus taught the same principle in John 15:22, declaring that if He, the Light of the world, had not come and exposed the sin of the world, they would have not realized their spiritual condition. Romans 7:9 also states this same type of word. A lack of exposure will link the believer to the Pharisees, who sit up front for all to see, who for pretence or a covering up of the truth, make long prayers, yet inwardly have not cleaned the cup and are ravening wolves. The word translated "pretence" in Matthew 23:14 and Philippians 1:18, and "cloke" in John 15:22 and 1 Thessalonians 2:5 is all the same Greek word. From this we see that Paul could tell the Thessalonian assembly that he had not worn the cloke of covetousness, that inner desire and love of money, which is the root of all evil, not only because of his outward actions, but also because of the trying of his heart by God (1 Thessalonians 2:4).

1 Thessalonians 5:22–24

> Abstain from every form of evil. Now may the God of peace Himself sanctify you entirely; and may your spirit and soul and body be preserved complete, without blame at the coming of our Lord Jesus Christ. Faithful is He who calls you, and He also will bring it to pass. (NASB)

Philippians 1:9–10

> And this I pray, that your love may abound still more and more in real knowledge and all discernment, so that you may approve the things that are excellent in order to be sincere and blameless until the day of Christ. (NASB)

These verses relate the goal of any true working of God, whether it comes through teaching, preaching, or ministering in the Spirit. The goal is for the Body of Christ, individually in each person and together as the church, to be blameless, without blemish, spot, or wrinkle. Blameless in every realm of our soul and mind is a lofty goal; yet, the Lord Jesus Christ has invested His Spirit into the church for that very purpose. Like gold, the impurities and imperfections need to be brought to the surface and removed by the refiner's fire before the true beauty can be seen or realized.

1 Corinthians 14:20

Brethren, be not children in understanding: howbeit in malice be ye children, but in understanding be men. (KJV)

Ephesians 1:18

The eyes of your understanding being enlightened: that ye may know what is the hope of His calling and what the riches of the glory of His inheritance in the saints. (KJV)

2 Kings 6:17a

And Elisha prayed, and said, Lord, I pray Thee, open his eyes, that he may see. (KJV)

Acts 26:18

To open their eyes, and to turn them from darkness to light, and from the power of Satan unto God, that they may receive forgiveness of sins, and inheritance among them which are sanctified by faith that is in me. (KJV)

1 John 2:11

But he that hateth his brother is in darkness, and walketh in darkness, and knoweth not whither he goeth, because that darkness hath blinded his eyes. (KJV)

These verses proclaim a principle about the importance of what we see through the eyes of our understanding. These eyes include our imagination. Therefore, what we see through these eyes affects us tremendously. Adam and Eve realized this the hard way as their transgression caused their eyes of understanding to be opened to the carnal, natural realm as seen in Genesis 3:5 and 7. In verse seven, it says that when their eyes were opened, that they knew that they were naked. They had been naked all along or at least clothed with the glory but had no shame because they were not aware of their nakedness because their eyes had not been opened to that information. In fact, the word "knew" in the proper Hebrew usage means to "ascertain by seeing." To have experiential knowledge of something, you must be able to see it with your mind's eye, or imagination. Paul proved that in Ephesians 1:18, saying that to know God's calling and God's inheritance your eyes of understanding must be enlightened to those things. Upon seeking their own wisdom from the tree of the knowledge of good and evil, the light of the Spirit of God that dwelt within their minds was replaced by darkness, having their understanding darkened, being alienated from the life of God (Ephesians 4:18). Through the decay of spiritual death, human eyes of understanding became full of darkness and his spiritual perception became very dull. Therefore, until Jesus came and restored us, God's dealings with humanity were mostly comprehended through the physical realm because the ability to understand the spiritual realm that God lives in was void. But now we can know Christ and other people no longer after the flesh, but after the Spirit (2 Corinthians 5:16). Human rebellion causes us to seek this knowing of spiritual matters through our own psychic abilities or through occultism and has forgotten the warnings of Jesus to "take heed therefore that the light which is in thee be not darkness" (Luke 11:35, KJV).

In all the mentioned verses, we see these eyes of understanding, or our ability to have spiritual insight, in a similar context. You could correlate these eyes of understanding with the concept of revelation knowledge; where you not only mentally agree with God's Word, but you know it to be true. Both Paul and Elisha prayed for someone, that their eyes would be opened and enlightened to be able to clearly see things that were spiritually significant. In Paul's case, it was that the believers would know (notice the use of the word "know" and eyes being enlightened, just like Genesis 3:7) their calling and great inheritance. In Elisha's case, it was so that his servant would be comforted in knowing the angelic forces of God that were defending them against their enemies. In contrast, later, Elisha prayed that the enemies would be smitten with blindness. It is possible that this blindness or darkness was also in the eyes of understanding, not only in their physical sight. They blindly followed Elisha, with no comprehension of where they were going, although most of them knew the geography of the area very well. This is just like the spiritual condition described in 1 John 2:11. If we hate, then this hatred acts like black clouds around our spiritual eyes and we walk around in darkness, sometimes not even realizing what we are doing or where we are going or why we respond in certain ways. The men pursuing Elisha were so blinded concerning any comprehension that they did not even know that the man they were chasing was the one aimlessly leading them around. We as believers should be watchful over our own heart because in the New Testament the sin of hatred was likened to murder by Jesus in Matthew 5. It not only causes us to walk in darkness, but if left to grow in our heart, those seeds of hate could one day erupt into violence.

In our world today, people have darkened eyes of understanding, unable to clearly see the loving, concerned nature of God that they may have heard about all their lives. Through the root of bitterness, the enemy has blinded their minds eye from being able to see the light of the glorious gospel (2 Corinthians 4:4). They are children in understanding, which in the context of 1 Corinthians 14:20, can have an implied meaning of the feelings or the sensitive nature of a person. They are childish and darkened in their emotions, easily hurt, extremely sensitive, easily offended. Many times, these emotional issues manifest themselves through the dark, sullen physical eyes of the person, which is a complete contrast to the sparkling, radiating eyes of a person filled with God's life.

The appearances of Jesus to His disciples between the Resurrection and Pentecost are also related to this principle of opening the eyes of understanding. The Emmaus Road experience is found in Luke 24. In verse fifteen, there are two disciples walking and Jesus appearing and walking with them. The next verse says that their eyes were holden, so that they did not know Him. Obviously, it is speaking of their eyes of understanding. Again, as in Genesis 3:7 and Ephesians 1:18, the correlation of the word "know" and eyes of understanding is seen. That makes three biblical witnesses to the principle of opening the eyes of understanding to have true, tangible, experiential knowledge of a subject or person. The journey goes on with a time of Word teaching by the Lord expounding on the things of the Old Testament that show Him. But even with all this insight, their eyes of understanding are not fully opened. The Lord wants to press further, but many people do not want to make the efforts to be in these realms. Jesus will go in and tarry in that place (Luke 24:29), but I believe His perfect will would be to keep pressing further into the deep mysteries of God. This pressing can come through the experience of getting personal with Jesus, which in the Emmaus Road account is shown in the breaking of bread. As soon as Jesus gave them the bread, their eyes of understanding were opened, and they "knew" Him. This word, YADA in the Hebrew, can imply an intimate relationship, as Adam and Eve through the sexual relationship, or describing God's activity concerning His covenant with the children of Israel in Exodus 2:25. Great teaching and knowledge of the Word is an important part of our walk with Jesus, as He taught them in verse twenty-seven, but there is also a deeper walk where the eyes of understanding can be enlightened in greater depths than ever before. Your heart may burn within you as your spirit bears witness to the teaching of the Word, but unless your eyes are opened to their full extent the experiential knowledge of knowing Him may be dimmed. You must know, have your eyes of understanding opened, to the truth, for it to set you free (John 8:32). We can know Jesus after the Spirit in greater dimensions than those who walked with Him after the flesh (2 Corinthians 5:16). In the case of the two disciples, their eyes were opened, and Jesus became "known" to them in the breaking of bread. Sharing a meal is a covenant experience that

Jesus promised for the one who would open the door of his heart to receive the chastening and reproving of the Lord in a zealous manner (Revelation 3:19–20). Mary Magdalene, who had received previous deliverance from demons, had her eyes opened by the resurrected Lord speaking her name. Another instance shows a group of disciples having their eyes opened through supernatural provision of Jesus (John 21:1–14). In Paul's instructions about behavior at the Lord's table, he speaks of the believer examining and judging ourselves. Careless participation in the life of God can cause sickness and premature death. The Lord would prefer us to examine and try our hearts and allow Him to cleanse the inward heart.

Full inheritance includes the eyes being opened plus the rejoicing of the heart (Psalms 19:8). This enlightening of the eyes comes from the nail in a sure place (Ezra 9:8) that Isaiah saw having the key of David to shut and open the access to the throne of judgment (Isaiah 22:23), Who as One Shepherd (Ecclesiastes 12:11), He alone has the words of delight that Solomon was seeking. Between his anointing to be king and his philosophical study in Ecclesiastes, Solomon forgot that he had received this wisdom to judge and understand the heart of people as a gift from God. The ability to minister the grace and the counsel of the Lord is an anointing from the Spirit of God, not a knowledge learned from books. His enlightenment is the only thing that can take away the sorrow and depression that causes suicide and death (Psalms 13:2–3). His counsel is what can make glad and brighten up the heart (Psalms 16:7–9). "I sought the Lord and He heard me and delivered me from all my fears. They looked unto Him, and were enlightened, and their faces were not ashamed (Psalms 34:5, KJV).

2 Samuel 13:18–19

> And she had a garment of divers colours upon her: for with such robes were the king's daughters that were virgins appareled. Then his servant brought her out

and bolted the door after her. And Tamar put ashes on her heart and rent her garment of divers colours that was on her, and laid her hand on her head, and went on crying. (KJV)

Isaiah 61:3

To appoint unto them that mourn in Zion, to give unto them beauty for ashes, the oil of joy for mourning, the garment of praise for the spirit of heaviness; that they might be called trees of righteousness, the planting of the Lord, that He might be glorified. (KJV)

Psalms 51:17–18

Do good in Thy good pleasure unto Zion; build Thou the walls of Jerusalem. (KJV)

All these verses are dealing with the restoration of God for the sexually abused. Greater than any other, the trauma and spiritual consequences of the sexually abused are indeed a tremendous affliction from the enemy. The first verse from 2 Samuel is the first and the last we hear of Tamar, a daughter of King David. She is raped by her brother, Ammon, and then cast away by him. After being raped and no longer having the prize of virginity, Tamar rips off her royal apparel, feeling unworthy to wear such clothing, even though her purity had been stolen from her. She put ashes on her head as a sign of mourning and continued this existence of self-abuse her whole life. Her only counsel came from Absalom, who told her to stop crying and not to let it bother her, or as the Hebrew says, let it set in your heart. The church has a history of this same style of counseling for the sexually abused. This counsel did not lead or help her to overcome the situation and she remained in Absalom's house, desolate, alone, and ruined. A time of trauma, which may have lasted no longer than thirty minutes, would affect the rest of her entire life.

In verse thirteen of the same chapter, Tamar asks Ammon a question. The abused are asking the same question. In the New American Standard, it reads this way; "As for me, where could I get rid of my reproach?" The death or imprisonment of the abuser has limited healing effect because Ammon was killed by Absalom a couple of years after the rape. The wrath of humanity, although necessary for good society and order, cannot bring about the righteousness of God (James 1:20).

The promise of God to the sexually abused is found in the prophetic verses about the ministry of the Messiah. There is an antidote for each response that Tamar lived out. In response to the ashes on her head, Isaiah prophesied that Messiah would bring to her beauty. The ashes were not only a sign of mourning but also to darken or mask the face of the person. Messiah brings to the abused His beauty in place of the feelings of filthiness and ugliness. In response to the mourning and crying, Messiah brings the oil of joy. In response to the casting away of the virgin apparel, Messiah brings the garment of praise that will also drive away the spirit of heaviness. In Psalms 69:20, it declares how Jesus experienced all the reactions that Tamar had, knowing disgrace, reproach, shame, a broken heart, heaviness, and the lonely feelings that there is no one to take pity and comfort. Jesus the Messiah has experientially identified Himself with the pain and abuse of the sexually abused and desires to heal the lives of the mourners in Zion, that God may be glorified. Jesus said in John 20:21, "As Father hath sent Me, even so send I you" (KJV). Jesus was sent to heal the brokenhearted, even so, He sends us to do the same. The counsel of Absalom, who may meet the physical need of food and shelter, lacks the spiritual understanding to meet the needs of the wounded heart.

The 51st Psalm is another witness to the need of renewal from sexual sin, being David's prayer after being compelled to deal with his sin with Bathsheba by a revealing word of a prophet. This Psalm could link with sexual abuse because there are times when the victims may end up living lives of promiscuity, seeking affection and love in ways of ungodliness. The unclean spirits that were transferred from the abuse will attempt to lead them further into the pit of despair. In verse six of the Psalm, a little bit of inner healing terminology is used, where David says, "Behold, Thou dost desire truth in the innermost being, and in the hidden part Thou wilt make me know wisdom" (KJV). The process of the creation of a clean heart to the restoring the joy of salvation all point to a work of God in the heart. It is God's desire (pleasure) to rebuild the walls of our heart to connect us with His pleasure to give us the kingdom. In conjunction with Psalms 147:2–3, it admonishes that this rebuilding is done through a ministry of healing the heart from its sorrows and griefs. God wants to arise and build these walls as part of the restoration work of His kingdom.

IX

God Will Arise

Nehemiah 2:20

> Then answered I them, and said unto them, 'the God of heaven, He will prosper us; therefore, we His servants will arise and build: but ye have no portion, nor right, nor memorial, in Jerusalem.' (KJV)

Malachi 4:2

> But unto you that fear My name shall the Sun of righteousness arise with healing in His wings; and ye shall go forth and grow up as calves of the stall. (KJV)

Most Bible people understand the book of Nehemiah to be a type and a shadow of the workings of God within the soul of a people, to restore and rebuild broken down walls. It is my conviction that inner healing prayer ministry is a major part of the new covenant fulfillment of this principle. Through other Scriptural references, this discourse has shown how the activity of God arising correlates with the principles of the inner healing message.

In Nehemiah chapter two, Nehemiah is doing his duties for the king. One day, when he went before the king, his countenance was notably sad. The king recognized his situation as sorrow of heart, sorrow for his beloved city, which was in ruins. This is a type and a shadow of Jesus, the believer's high priest, going before the Father, interceding on our behalf. Since He experienced our weaknesses for Himself, Jesus desires to bear the burden and terminate abuse within His body. He met Saul face-to-face on the road to Damascus on behalf of His persecuted people. From the spiritual side paralleling what is going on with Nehemiah, The Lord Jesus has a heavy heart in seeing the walls of trust, acceptance, hope and love in ruins amongst the personalities of His people. The only sensible plan is to rebuild the walls. In verse ten, there are two men who are representative of both the enemy and those who fail to see the need for all this time and prayer effort, and careful concern to nurture the bruised back to life. Verses twelve and sixteen are important to me personally, as it symbolizes Jesus coming to start a rebuilding work in my life and telling no one about it, especially me. At that time, I was studying about deliverance and demons and the whole concept about demonic activity within the believer's life. I knew nothing about inner healing until that prayer group night that the presence of the Lord touched me, and I opened my heart and expressed my love for the Savior. Then the next few years, he rebuilt the walls of my heart through specific prayer ministry. It is marvelous to know that the secret things still belong to the Lord and that God may bring a new revelation to see if we will receive it through the faith of the moment and the demonstration of His Spirit, knowing that He will confirm His actions to us through the written Word as we search for it.

The last three verses of chapter two are a key in this specific principle. In response to Nehemiah's request to rebuild the walls, the workers, who on this side of the cross are the intercessors who co-labor with God in prayer for the broken, say the phrase that this study has revolved around, "let us rise up and build." Since we co-labor with God's Spirit, if we say we will arise, it is because God has already spoken it before, and we obey His command. Then in verse twenty, there needs to be an answer to the adversaries who come out to persecute and laugh. The God of heaven will shower His blessing upon this rebuilding work so that our adversaries will have no portion (allotment, part) right (demonic strongholds legally operating in our lives through generational sin) or memorial (record, memento) in the city of our heart. This rebuilding work needs to be a complete work, and if we allow Him access, He that begins this good work will fully accomplish it. The importance of combating the generational sin principle is strongly seen in the life of King David. Because of his adultery and murder, the sword never departed from his house and eventually evil rose up out of his own house (2 Samuel 12:10–11). Ammon, David's son, had an incestuous affair with Tamar. Absalom, another son, ended up killing Ammon. Absalom sought to take the kingdom for himself. He also had sexual relations with ten of his father's concubines, openly before all of Israel, which God prophesied because David had tried to cover up his sin. Even the beloved son of the Lord, Solomon, because of a weakness for women, had the kingdom rent from him in the generation of his son. On and on the curse will go unless we appropriate specifically through prayer the power of the blood of Jesus to the weakness of our past generations.

The rest of the book of Nehemiah continues with the theme of restoration. In chapter four there are the same enemies from chapter two trying to disrupt the work they were unable to stop earlier. God will bring to nothing the ungodly counsel (Nehemiah 4:15, Psalms 33:10), that the true thoughts of His heart; deliverance, healing, and freedom may be made known to all generations (Psalms 33:11). The margin reference in the New American Standard says the HEALING of the walls.

Name definitions and the activity of that period continue to illuminate these principles. The definition of Nehemiah is "consolation of Jah, to comfort and console one in distress." The same Greek word is used for both advocate in 1 John 2:1 and comforter in John 14. Therefore, Jesus calls the Holy Spirit another comforter (John 14:16), because the Lord Jesus Christ Himself is a comforter, consoler, advocate, etc. Nehemiah proves to be the Old Testament type and shadow of this work of God to arise and rebuild and his name bears witness to this as well. Another interesting reference point is that the prophet Malachi was speaking and prophesying during the time of Nehemiah. This is important because Malachi speaks of things that portray inner healing language. The refiner and purifier in chapter three burns away the dross to show forth the pure metal. Further on the Lord lists who He will testify against; sorcerers, adulterers, false swearers, those who oppress the worker, the widow and the fatherless, and those who will not help the stranger. Jesus also pronounced judgment on that final group in Matthew 25:43. Although final judgment is not until the return of Jesus, through prayer, the believer can be acquitted from the bitterness of their own heart through the healing of the Holy Spirit.

Malachi is also the one who prophesied the anointing that would restore the heart relationship between fathers and their children. The Sun of righteousness will arise with healing. Like the natural sun at the dawning of a new day, the Sun of righteousness, our shield (Psalms 84:11), will arise to produce the work of this restoration and healing within the family. It may be darkest before the dawn, but God, Whose going forth is prepared as the morning (Hosea 6:3), will arise with the brilliance of the sunrise to bring healing to those tired from the weary night of the soul. Verses from Psalms proclaim this principle of the morning-healing correlation. In Psalms 30, where in verses two and three the writer cries for the deliverance and healing of his soul, it shares in verse five: "For His anger is but for a moment, His favor is for a lifetime: weeping may last for the night, but a shout of joy comes in the morning" (NASB). In Psalms 49:14–15, the Scripture declares: "like sheep they (corrupt man) are laid in the grave; death shall feed on them; and the upright shall have dominion over them *in the morning*: and their beauty shall consume in the grave from their dwelling. But God will redeem my soul from the hand of the grave: for He shall receive me. Selah" (KJV). In Psalms 46, it speaks of the Holy Spirit, the river of life who brings gladness to the city of God, as abundantly available for help. God provides help from trouble when the morning dawns, or when the morning appears. In Psalms 143:8, when David's spirit was overwhelmed and fainting, he desired to hear the lovingkindness of the Lord in the morning.

Like Nehemiah's special construction project, God makes special provision for those who have been abused by other people and the enemy. In Genesis 29, it shows that God saw that Leah, Jacob's wife, was hated. Jacob wanted Rachel but got Leah first because of Laban's deception. In verse thirty-one, it says that when the Lord saw that Leah was hated, He opened her womb to bear children to Jacob, but Rachel was barren. Although more beautiful by physical means, Rachel became envious of her sister. Leah was not well-favored like Rachel in body, but God showed her special favor because He has pity or compassion for those who are afflicted by others. After the resurrection, Jesus made similar provision for Peter by making sure to specifically speak his name when calling for the disciples. The wounded heart's special provision is the prayer ministry of others for the healing of memories, which also came to Peter as the sun arose that morning. It is no coincidence that this same Peter in one of his epistles writes in encouragement to the believer to give attention to the prophetic word of the Scripture, "until the day breaks through the gloom and the Morning Star rises (comes into being) in your hearts" (2 Peter 1:19, Amplified Bible). Since the sun is characterized as a star, Peter had come to know the sun arising in his heart just like Malachi had prophesied it hundreds of years before, as a process of healing and the burning up of the roots of the enemy. Jesus said in Revelation 22:16 that He is that Bright and Morning Star, the Sun of righteousness that shines in brilliant splendor, invading the darkness in people's hearts, to heal and transform them. Revelation 2:23 and 28 correlate into one group those who receive the message of the searching of the heart and the trying of the reins with the receiving of the morning star, the healing Sun of righteousness. The promises of Scripture may remain darkened until the sun arises in the heart with healing. The entrance of the Word brings light, but hatred or strife in the heart, especially the secret heart, can choke that Word and that light, causing the believer to remain in darkness, with their eyes of understanding darkened.

God will arise. A vital phrase for this study. In the Word of God, there are two main activities of God that show out from God arising. He arises to go to His resting place or place of honor, and to judge. He goes to His throne and sits down as the Judge of all the earth.

In Numbers 10:35, it says, "Rise up O Lord! And let Thine enemies be scattered and let those who hate Thee flee before Thee" (NASB). At that time, the children of Israel were looking for a resting place for themselves and for the ark of the covenant. They knew that they would have rest if they stayed in the presence of God. This rising of God was also for them to go forth in victory, as God's enemies are scattered before Him. We also see a similar type of prayer in the dedication ceremony of the temple that Solomon built. In 2 Chronicles 6:41, Solomon prayed, "Now therefore, Arise, O Lord God, to Thy resting place, Thou and the ark of Thy might; let Thy priests, O Lord God, be clothed with salvation, and let Thy godly ones rejoice in what is good" (NASB). This same prayer is found in Psalms 132:8.

When God sits down in His place of honor, He is still active. He never sleeps nor slumbers and is never at a loss for energy. There always comes forth a purpose to this action of God. He does not move idly or speak forth idle words. His actions are not vain or without purpose. God sits down in His place of honor for the purpose of judgment. In the lives of the afflicted and abused, this is not judgment as in wrath, but is judgment as in justice. God is a righteous judge, and His judgments are true.

The book of Psalms is full of verses that show this concept of God arising on behalf of the afflicted to do justice. These verses can manifest in an experiential way through inner healing prayer.

Psalms 3:7

> Arise O Lord; save me O my God. For You have struck all my enemies on the cheek; You have broken the teeth of the ungodly. (Amplified Bible)

God's actions of arising always carries the workings of warfare and deliverance along with it. David wrote this Psalm when Absalom was seeking to destroy him and the kingdom. Although thousands before had revolted against him and thousands were with Absalom, David did not let the betrayal of his son and the people weaken his faith in God because he declared that God would arise on his behalf.

Psalms 7:6

> Arise O Lord, in your anger; lift up Yourself against the rage of my enemies; and awake and stir up for me the justice and vindication that You have commanded. (Amplified Bible)

Psalms 35:23–24

> Arouse Yourself, awake to the justice due me, even to my cause, my God and my Lord. Judge and vindicate me, O Lord my God, according to Your righteousness, Your righteous and justice; and let my foes not rejoice over me. (Amplified Bible)

God is a God of justice and righteousness. Righteousness and justice are the foundation of His throne (Psalms 89:14). Therefore, He desires truth and justice to prevail. In God's court system, the guilty and wicked are not acquitted, unless they repent. He has commanded justice and vindication for the afflicted. In David's cry for help in the first reference verse, this justice would come because of God arising. In the second reference is a similar cry for help so that the enemies would not even have a victory. The enemy rejoices when we as believers do not take our case against him before the Judge of all the earth because God can be limited in His ability to help us unless we pray.

Psalms 9:4,6,18,19

> For You have maintained my right and my cause; You
> sat on the throne judging righteously. The enemy
> have been cut off and have vanished in everlasting
> ruins, You have plucked up and overthrown their
> cities; the very memory of them has perished and
> vanished. For the needy shall not always be forgotten,
> and the expectation and hope of the meek and the
> poor shall not perish forever. Arise, O Lord! Let not
> man prevail; let the nations be judged before You.
> (Amplified Bible)

All these verses tie together the concepts of God arising to bring
justice and to maintain the rights and plead the cause of His people,
thereby destroying even the memory of the enemy's work. The whole
passage of Psalms 9 could be in this reference. Verse seven says that
God has prepared His throne for judgment. Verse nine declares
God to be a refuge for the oppressed. Verse twelve shows that God
avenges the shedding of innocent blood and remembers the cry of
the afflicted. Truly, the Lord's heart is toward the oppressed and the
afflicted and through specific healing prayer opportunities, He can
turn the mourning into dancing.

Psalms 10:12,14,17,18

> Arise O Lord! O God, lift up Your hand; forget not
> the humble (patient and crushed). You have seen it;
> yes, You note trouble and grief (vexation) to requite it
> with Your hand. The unfortunate commits himself to
> You; You are the helper of the fatherless. O Lord, You
> have heard the desire and the longing of the humble
> and the oppressed; You will prepare and strengthen
> and direct their hearts, You will cause Your ear to

hear, to do justice to the fatherless and the oppressed, so that man, who is of the earth, may not terrify them anymore. (Amplified Bible)

These verses contain much of the inner healing message concisely. God does not note or keep track of sin after it has been confessed, but He certainly does call to record trouble and grief that wounded the heart. Through God arising, He seeks to requite this vexation by giving pay-back to the enemy. If the fatherless and the oppressed will fully and completely commit themselves and all their troubles to God the Father, He promises to be their helper and deliverer while also strengthening and redirecting their hearts and lives. These actions make sure that the enemy does not have any more hold and cannot cause fear anymore.

Psalms 12:5

Now will I arise, says the Lord, because the poor are oppressed, because of the groans of the needy; I will set him in safety and in the salvation for which he pants. (Amplified Bible)

Psalms 17:13

Arise O Lord! Confront and forestall them, cast them down! Deliver my life for the wicked by Your sword. (Amplified Bible)

Psalms 68:1

God is already beginning to arise, and His enemies to scatter; let them also who hate Him flee before Him! (Amplified Bible)

This 68th Psalm makes other references to this message of deliverance from the enemy, which is a theme that connects all these references. The 17th Psalm speaks of God confronting the enemies. Healing prayer and deliverance commands is the Spirit of God openly confronting the powers of darkness that hold believers in bondage. This open display can be necessary for freedom to come forth. The rest of Psalm 68 also declares God as a father of the fatherless and the judge and protector of the widow. Those who have had husbands and fathers stolen from them through death or abuse are precious in the sight of God and He seeks to show Himself strong on their behalf.

Psalms 74:21–22

> Oh, let not the downtrodden return in shame; let the oppressed and needy praise Your name. Arise, O God, plead Your own cause; remember earnestly how the foolish and impious man scoffs and reproaches you day after day and all the day long. (Amplified Bible)

Psalms 82:3,4,8

> Do justice to the weak (poor) and fatherless; maintain the rights of the afflicted and needy. Deliver the poor and needy; rescue them out of the hand of the wicked. Arise, O God, judge the earth! For to You belong all the nations. (Amplified Bible)

These verses again request God to do a work of bringing justice to the fatherless and deliverance to the needy through God arising to judge. God, as a righteous judge, commands restitution for a victim.

In Numbers 6:26, there is the blessing that the priests were to use in blessing the people of God. This blessing seems to fit in with this theme from Psalms. It declares, "the Lord lift up His approving countenance upon you and give you peace (tranquility of heart) and life continually" (Amplified Bible). The action of lifting up His countenance is another way of saying that God is arising. God arises with healing that bears the fruit of peace within the heart. Peace does not come from formulas or programs. Ephesians 2:14 declares that Jesus Christ Himself is our peace. Whether that peace is between nations, people, families or within our own heart, Jesus is the Prince of peace and His presence alone is what is needed.

God arises on behalf of the afflicted, oppressed, downtrodden, the fatherless, the widow and the orphan. He arises against the enemies of His people, to scatter them and destroy them. Another reference from Psalms 68 is ideal for these concepts. In verse six, it declares, "God setteth the solitary in families: He bringeth out those which are bound with chains: but the rebellious dwell in a dry land" (KJV). The afflicted, fatherless, widow and oppressed very often experience the loneliness and solitary life that the verse speaks about. The rejected become self-rejectors, and deep down believe that everyone else will reject them. But God has a solution. The answer is the restoration work of the Holy Spirit. In John 14:18, Jesus said, "I will not leave you comfortless: I will come to you" (KJV). The reference in the margin says that comfortless could be translated "as orphans." God understands the feelings that would have arisen if Jesus would have left the earth and left the disciples on their own, without any help. Their wanderings before the day of Pentecost show this path. Their witness would have been powerless. Orphans and the fatherless have this rejection within them. Just like the power of the Holy Spirit transformed followers who were running and hiding for fear of their lives into bold and powerful witnesses, that same power can transform the rejected, fearful heart of a child into a loving and fearless one. The promise of Psalms 68 is that God will set these solitary ones, those who are alone and helpless, in families. The definition of the Hebrew word translated families is "a house where building takes place, to repair." The house, of course, is the body of Christ, where God has placed people and ministries that work to repair and rebuild broken lives. Although in the physical realm, those who wound others are not always brought to justice, God Almighty, the Judge of all the earth, has commanded justice for the afflicted and oppressed. He sees them becoming guilty of bitterness and hatred in their hearts for those who have wounded them. These can bring torment into their own hearts. He will arise on their behalf, with healing, justice, and vindication, thereby transforming the wounds and the pains of the past. This spiritual restitution will then enable them to seek true physical and emotional restitution, not in vengeance or wrath, but with love and forgiveness. The intercession, confrontation, and release that comes through healing prayer for the inner heart is a vital part of this process. He patiently waits for the wounded to seek Him out and experience Him in these realms.

X

Epilogue

As we get close to the finish line, there are some verses and principles that may not have fit well with the other major themes in this study, but, nevertheless, should be part of this research. I want to also summarize a few personal observations from having received ministry over the years and have begun to learn some navigational tools surrounding the soul of a person. Research and insight need to be appropriated into the life of the believer in a practical way.

The Christian life is a lifetime journey that should involve the transformation and healing of the soul so that the purity of the spirit has a clean vessel to manifest through in the earth. This spirit, who has been clothed with the righteousness of God, has become the residence of the Holy Spirit. Although this spirit has received the life of God and he is born from above, 2 Corinthians 7:1 declares that it can become defiled or contaminated if it is continually subjected to unclean things. We are saved, but not yet glorified, and the unclean things of this earthly experience can still influence the believer if they yoke themselves to darkness. The care and nurture of this spirit, from the mother's womb and throughout life, is vital. Although reference to the location of the spirit being the belly is common, the spirit permeates the entire being, for it is the spirit that gives life to the body.

James 2:26 says that the body without the spirit is dead. Residing in this spirit is the conscience, the inner knowledge of right and wrong, the guiding element within our being. This spirit, although perfected, still must function through the soul. A preacher, although anointed to preach, will speak through their personality. The personality will manifest in this physical realm through the actions of the body. Our triune being, spirit, soul, and body, is representative of God Himself as well as the Old Testament temple with the holy of holies, holy place, and outer court. To experience the manifest presence of God, the veil of the self-life must be transformed. Anointing and personality are not the same thing. A loud person will be a loud preacher; a quiet person, although speaking with all the boldness of the Spirit, will still likely be quiet. These differences do not offend God as He made people different for His purposes, but the offence comes when there are demonic things in our personalities that circumvent the plan and purpose of God. Eagerness to begin ministry without the timing of God, following the spontaneity of the soul without the patience of the spirit, can cause embarrassment to the preacher and thwart the plan of God. The body of Christ is witness of some ministers, after becoming known by millions, while never confronting the enemy within their own being, who had the enemy show out from the dormant stage of the soul to cause scandal and unrighteousness that also allowed the enemies of the Lord to blaspheme. The better timing of God may be to do a searching work in our lives and get all the darkness out and then send us forth in the anointing of the Spirit. Even Jesus, Who had no darkness in His soul, was not sent forth into ministry until He defeated the temptations of the enemy through the Word. If the soul is not transformed and the darkness is not removed, the full glory of God will not be able to shine through. An unrenewed soul will act out in rebellion and complain in the time of trials and testing, falling away into the wilderness, and never seeing the full promise. The new wine of the life of God must be put into the fresh wineskins. The saving of the soul is necessary, in both areas of conscious and subconscious thought, so that both spirit and soul can be preserved. If the old wineskins are nor repaired or replaced, then the new wine of the life in the Spirit will spill out onto the ground, becoming useless and contaminated because the container was not able to contain the glory of the new wine. The wounds of rejection, abuse and fear act like rips and tears in the wineskins of our soul and the healing stitch of the Holy Spirit is the only thing that can permanently sew back together the torn and broken heart (Psalms 147:3). Unless the whole of our being is refined by God, the dysfunctional aspects of any wounded area of the heart will influence and hinder the flow of the Spirit of God through our lives. We cannot completely develop and strengthen our spirit without also transforming and healing the soul.

As I was thinking about how we should receive this healing, I thought of a way that would be the opposite of God's methods – the process of osmosis from the efforts of others. Osmosis is defined as "an apparently effortless absorption of ideas, feelings and attitudes." That so truthfully describes how many people try and receive from God. They want to sit idly by and over the decades of life hope the blessing will somehow slide their way or otherwise let someone else intercede and labor in the Spirit for them. This type of believer may receive a little restoration from the work of others, but they will be unable to keep the blessing because the enemy steals the word from those who have little roots of their own. The faith of God is full of activity to be done by the believer and permanent and lasting results are found through consistent, personal faith and prayer. James 5:16 specifically speaks of this confession and prayer concerning the inner person. The effect of this activity is "that you may be healed and restored to a spiritual tone of mind and heart" (Amplified Bible).

The inner heart needs this work of God because of the destructive work of the enemy in their life. We can see this progression through the example of the life of Judas. In John 13:2, it says, "and supper being ended, the devil having now put into the heart of Judas Iscariot, Simon's son, to betray Him" (KJV). The enemy's entrance into a life usually comes through and is initiated from the heart and thought life. In John 12:6, we read that Judas was a thief, thereby allowing the enemy access into his life. When the thought of betrayal of Jesus came, a choice had to be made by him. Like Judas, we either receive the thought and allow the seed to grow or we can cast down the thought that is not in obedience to Jesus Christ. The believer's decision is the determining factor in how much effect the seed has in their life, as the seed is sown all over, but its effectiveness depends on the soil. In Luke 22:3, it declares, "then entered Satan into Judas named Iscariot" (KJV). Judas had made a covenant with the chief priests and sought opportunity to conduct the plan, according to Matthew 26:15–16. This part of the process is the conceiving or bringing to birth of the deed. Psalms 7:14 speaks of the wicked person conceiving, being pregnant and giving birth to iniquity. This is what Judas was doing by seeking opportunity and speaking about the betrayal and gave the enemy a wide-open door into his life to operate through him. The mercy of God and the intercessory covering of others may keep the door closed off for a while but a person who is persistent in giving place to the enemy will eventually reap that spiritual harvest of destruction. This process of the birthing of the action within the heart can give the enemy the same level of access as the doing of the action accomplishes. When Judas took the piece of bread from Jesus at the Passover meal, John 13:27 says that the enemy entered him again, just like earlier in Luke 22. We need to understand that conceiving sin in the heart will give the enemy the same access and influence that doing the sin does later. This conceiving in the heart, especially in the life of a child, may not be seen or noticed in the physical realm until the complete action is done, but it is going on. The disciples at the table did not know what was happening until the actual betrayal in the garden of Gethsemane. But, after the empowerment of the Holy Spirit, Peter, through the word of knowledge, knew of the evil deed concerning Ananias and Sapphira before it became evident. This same exposure can happen to the believer today; yet, for our benefit, lest we be brought under the judgment of God without the intervention of mercy.

This concept of exposing the workings of the evil, unbelieving heart in a believer (Hebrews 3:12) before the complete and full circle of consequences comes forth is the heart of the inner healing message. Even Judas earnestly sought for a way out after realizing the full effect of his betrayal, but the very ones whose position granted them to provide this way out turned him away and he was left alone to bear the consequence of his sin.

In Matthew 5:17, Jesus proclaims that He came to fulfill the law. In doing so, His new commandment takes the law one step further and is not to be a mere outward observance but is to also be an inward change. Christian maturity needs to be more than just a putting away of the action of sin but should also find out the roots behind certain actions. In speaking about the sixth commandment, Jesus begins to carry it even further than the physical act of murder. 1 John 3:14–15 also reiterates this principle and declares that in the New Covenant that hatred is the same as murder. The New Covenant declares that we do not merely look at the action of murder but seek to rid the human heart of the root of hatred. In Matthew 5:22, Jesus declares: "but I say to you that everyone who is angry with his brother shall be guilty before the court; and whoever shall say to his brother, Raca, shall be guilty before the supreme court; and whoever shall say, 'You fool" shall be guilty enough to go into the fiery hell" (NASB). Being angry and speaking insultingly without cause is the same as murder under the New Testament law of love. Even thinking these types of things can carry spiritual weight. Ecclesiastes 10:20 exhorts, "Curse not the king, no not even in your thoughts, and curse not the rich in your bedchamber, for a bird of the air will carry the voice, and a winged creature will tell the matter" (Amplified Bible). Although it is unlikely that the enemy of our soul can effectively read our thoughts, somehow our thoughts do have a discernible voice or substance in that realm that is accessible to him. It is apparent that the use of the word bedchamber can imply about the subconscious area of the thoughts. Solomon used this terminology in Proverbs, Ecclesiastes, and Song of Solomon to speak of an innermost, secret place. Therefore, the implication of cursing someone in your secret heart is clear. The birds that carry this are the same as the fowls of the air from the parable of the sower and those who Abraham fought off in Genesis 15 as they came to steal the sacrifice he had readied to give to God. These secret thoughts give access to our lives to the enemy to continually influence our behavior and hinder the blessing of God. James 1:15 speaks of lust being conceived and then bringing forth the fruit of sin. Sin, specifically hatred in these cases, is a by-product of an evil heart.

In Matthew 5:23, there is a resolution to this situation. Jesus declares, "Therefore" (*as a result of the pending judgment for the angry and bitter in heart*) "if thou bring thy gift to the altar, and there rememberest that thy brother hath ought against thee; leave there thy gift before the altar and go thy way; first be reconciled to thy brother, and then come and offer thy gift" (KJV). Reconciliation between you and influential people in your life is a principal factor that affects your relationship with God. The word translated "ought" in the King James means something or anything at all, so it does not have to be horrendous wounding that has occurred to affect the heart. Little children are hurt at the slightest of things. Weakness in the conscience makes wounding that conscience simple. Once the revelation of the heart condition has come, it is foremost important to deal with it as Jesus taught so that we can return and offer praise to God from a pure heart. Malachi 3:3 speaks of this as the refiner and purifier purging the people so that their offering may be offered in complete righteousness.

In returning to Judas, we see that he had walked with the disciples for three years, seeing the miracles, hearing the preaching, and had obtained a part of the ministry. In Acts 1:20, Peter speaks of the necessity of having someone else who had traveled with them and been a witness of the resurrection to take his place, which God prophesied in Psalms 109:8, "and let another take his office" (KJV). In seeking God about who this should be, the disciples spoke about God knowing the hearts of all. They saw that they had been blind to this condition concerning Judas. They had learned that an evil heart, although not always identifiable just by human understanding, could be someone's ruin. So, they desired to entrust the selection process to the Lord, Who can search the heart. The vessels of dishonor must be purged out so that the Master can use us in a mighty way.

Although wounds and abuse should never be used as an excuse

to completely rationalize our own decision to sin, there is benefit in searching hearts and minds for roots of destruction that are used by the enemy and the uninformed soul to overwhelm the believer. People rarely lose the control of their being overnight; it is a prolonged process of decay that started with an event that gave place of influence to the enemy. In Matthew 27:3, the Amplified Bible says that "Judas was afflicted in mind and troubled for his former folly." The result of his opening the door to the enemy was not only the action of sin but was then the torment and affliction in his memories. In the case of the abused, the memories of their abuse are like a constantly running movie that will not shut off.

Whether it was with repentance or just remorse for the consequences in his heart, Judas took the wages of his sin back to the priests and elders. These men were supposed to be ministers of the grace of God but corruptness in their own heart enabled them to have no compassion for him. This corruption did not necessarily void the anointing they should have been operating in to help him because John 11 records Caiaphas prophesying about one man dying for the whole nation and Eli the priest knew it was the Lord speaking to young Samuel. Yet, they left Judas to wallow in his sin and guilt and bad memories all alone. Knowing that all was lost, he became under the control of a suicide spirit and went out and ended his life. It shudders the spirit to think in parallel of how many people have sought out ministry for their soul and were instead left alone to fight their battle. They may be believers caught in bondage to guilt and painful memories or unbelievers caught in despair seeking refuge. Regardless of who they are or what the situation is, the Prince of peace desires to be the source of help in their time of trouble. Even in the Old Testament, the person who unintentionally killed someone was given a place of refuge to hide in until a fair trial could be undertaken, and true justice served (Numbers 35, Deuteronomy 19, Joshua 20). In parallel, New Testament believers, as a holy priesthood, should allow the one whose hatred and bitterness come from wounds of their past, a place of refuge, a place to hide in from the destructive effects that they are sowing. This will allow them a chance to rethink the condition of their heart and a chance to change and repent. In the Old Testament city of refuge, the one running for shelter was to go to this appointed city and the people were to give them refuge from the revenger of blood. The church of the Lord Jesus Christ is now, in this dispensation, to be this appointed city that people run into for shelter. Without this covering of prayer and spiritual warfare, the tormentors will eventually hunt down and catch that one who continues to carry unforgiveness in their heart. This parallel is consistent with the Word because under the new covenant our anger and hatred, sometimes done ignorantly or without knowing the roots of it, are the same as murder. In the Old Testament, the person was to stay in the protection of the city of refuge until the death of the high priest. Jesus Christ, our high priest, Who understands our weaknesses, enables us to be protected in His church and then can return to possess our land without fear of the revenger of blood. If the believer comes out from under that protection too soon, there is opportunity for the revenger of blood to slay them. It seems proper that the anger and hatred that is sown into a life from abuse and rejection would fall under the category of unawares (Joshua 20:3), ignorantly (Deuteronomy 19:4), and by error (Numbers 35:11). Since we are presently under a better covenant with better promises, the people of God should be offering to the abused with unintentional anger a better refuge and protection from their enemies.

From the Deuteronomy account of the city of refuge there is a concept that brings merit to the inner healing message. Deuteronomy 19:6 declares: "lest the avenger of blood pursue the slayer, while his heart is hot, and overtake him, because the way is long, and slay him, whereas he was not worthy of death, inasmuch as he hated him not in time past" (KJV). The type of killing in the Old Testament, which is akin to hatred and anger in the New, that is not a capital crime worthy of death, is the accidental or unintentional act or emotion that was not premeditated. Those people abused by family members or close friends did not hate them from the beginning- but continual abuse causes initial seeds of hate to grow and mature. Their hatred is not necessarily worthy of death because it is partly a human response to abuse and not premeditated, but nevertheless, the revenger of blood seeks to destroy them. Paul addressed this type of situation in Ephesians 6:4 and Colossians 3:21. In Colossians, he admonishes, "Fathers, provoke not your children to anger, lest they be discouraged" (KJV). In Ephesians, it says, "And, ye fathers, provoke not your children to wrath: but bring them up in the nurture and admonition of the Lord" (KJV). In Colossians, the word translated "discouraged" in the King James actually means to become disheartened, or as the Amplified renders it, "to break the spirit." In Ephesians, the phrase "provoke to wrath" is from one Greek word which is a direct opposite to the word that is used to describe the Holy Spirit as a comforter, consoler, and counselor. It signifies to be angry alongside someone in opposition to the Holy Spirit coming alongside to help us. The atmosphere of childhood has broken their spirit; the unintentional anger comes from the enemy continually feeding their heart fear and violence. The definition of the word "fault" in James 5:16 as "an unintentional error" brings even greater revelation on how to fight against this hatred that has come by error – through confession and healing prayer from others in the body of Christ.

This concept of sin "not worthy of death" is also shown in the New Testament to give further reference to the passage from Deuteronomy. In 1 John 5:16, it declares: "if any man see his brother sin a sin which is not unto death, he shall ask, and he shall give him life for them that sin not unto death. There is a sin unto death: I do not say that he shall pray for it" (KJV). Interpreting this Scripture from the other witness in Deuteronomy, "not unto death" refers to unintentional error and ignorant or unconscious sin, or sin that is forced upon us against our will (Deuteronomy 22:25–26). This would agree with the concept of James 5:16, apart from James speaking of the transgressor realizing their need of prayer on their own while John speaks of this happening through the revelation by another brother or sister by simple observation or a word of knowledge. Sin that is unto death is sin that is willfully done by a person although the reality of right and wrong is known, with no remorse and full acceptance of the consequences. Believers that blatantly transgress the law of God with no fear of judgment and an attitude of lasciviousness, pervert the grace of God (Jude vs 4). That sin is worthy of death and can result in spiritual deadness or coma. Numbers 15:23–31 speaks of this type of distinction of sin, telling the priest to offer forgiveness to those who sin in ignorance, but to cut off those who sin presumptuously, or as the Hebrew says, "with an open hand." The word used in Numbers 15:30 has the same root as words translated praise in Psalms, indicating obvious and open actions. Romans 1:32 also speaks of this, showing that not only is this type of sin worthy of death, but that knowing the decree of God and doing it anyway creates even greater judgment and condemnation to those involved, to the point that they then go and approve and consent with others who are doing the same things. Peter spoke of this in 2 Peter 2:20–22, stating that it would be better to not know the way of righteousness than to know it and be overcome by evil again. Concerning this sin unto death, John said not to pray for it. From the witness of Deuteronomy, the other type of sin, not worthy of death, may be unintentional and unawares, unconscious to the person doing it. They may be aware of the tormentors that are after them and realize they need the protection of the city of refuge. The process of protection from 1 John starts out by an action of asking. The word "ask" there is not speaking of requesting as a favor like the word "pray" at the end of verse sixteen, but instead means to "demand of something due." What is due the one who is guilty of unconscious sin in the heart? If the sin is a result of hurt or grief from the past, especially rooted from the actions of others against us, the something due is healing and restoration to correct the path of the afflicted. Demand in this sense is more boldness to proclaim the promises of God than a twisting of God's arm. You do not have to "touch God" to get Him to want to minister to the afflicted and the broken. His heart is always ready to pour out to them before they even come to Him for assistance. The second "he" in verse sixteen, in referring to the one who gives life to those who sin not unto death, should be capitalized, as it refers to God. We obviously do the asking and praying but God is the only One who can give life in place of death. The word "life" there is *zoe* in the Greek, meaning everlasting life or the life of God.

The influence of legacy or heritage is another concept to consider when finalizing the inner healing message as it relates to the unbelieving heart in a believer. Physical characteristics and a godly heritage are factors that all believers will agree with. Paul was quick to remind Timothy of the spiritual heritage of faith that he had received from his mother and grandmother. Deuteronomy 7:9 declares that the blessing of the covenant extends to a thousand generations. But there seems to be a cursed potential from our heritage as well. In Exodus 20:5, the cycle of generational curses, sin and weakness to sin is spoken of as God visiting the iniquity of the fathers upon the third and fourth generation, especially concerning idolatry and occult activities. The witness of the word of the covenant is that the weakness to certain evil and iniquity can be as much a part of a person's heritage as having brown eyes and blond hair. The spiritual and psychological heritage that a child receives is as sure of a fact as the physical. Sometimes these intermingle, as in the case of disease and mental health. The plague of miscarriage or barrenness may be a result of ungodly heritage as God's Word has promised the blessing of children for His people (Deuteronomy 7:14, Psalms 113:9). Proverbs 26:2 declares, "so the curse causeless shall not come" (KJV). If the curse is on our lives and we cannot discern a viable reason of sin, a cause could be an effect of specific generational curses. None of us can change our heritage, but through renunciation and prayer the effects and influences can be broken and thus we can stop these things from being passed onto future generations.

This concept of the effects of the law of sin and death influencing future generations, or even nations, is found in Scripture. 2 Samuel 21:1–9 speaks of a famine that had lasted for three years. Knowing that the curse without a cause would not happen, King David sought the face of God for discernment. God showed him a situation from the reign of King Saul. The effects of Saul's sin were being felt in the nation near the end of David's kingdom. When David made restitution for the Gibeonites, verse fourteen says that God was intreated for the land. The injustice and bloodshed had caused a curse to come upon the earth. Adam's sin also caused the ground to be cursed (Genesis 3:17). Achan sinned and the whole nation was cursed (Joshua 7). You do not sin alone; the effects of defilement are far-reaching. In Daniel 9:1-19, Daniel confessed the sin of his country as his own. Malachi prophesied that if the message of the Elijah prophets concerning the restoration of the father-children relationship is not received, that the earth would be smitten with a curse. This heritage of cursing needs to be replaced with the heritage of the servants of the Lord (Isaiah 54:17). Abraham's seed should be influenced by the heritage of Jacob (Isaiah 58:14). The subduing of our enemies is part of this heritage of Jacob; therefore, believers should be treading upon those evil high places, fortresses, and curses. Isaiah prophesied that these high places would fall in the day that the Lord healed the wounds and hearts of His people (Isaiah 30:25–26).

In Matthew 23, Jesus taught the religious leaders about the process of generational sin. These leaders were confident in their own righteousness and declared that if they had been in the previous generations with their ancestors that they surely would not have killed the prophets. Jesus, understanding their weakness toward spiritual bigotry, prophesied to them that they would not only perform at that level, but they would also complete and fully accomplish the measure of their fathers. In 1 Thessalonians 2:14 and 16, Paul spoke of the same situation. There were those persecuting the churches of God in Judea, who Paul likened to those who killed the Lord Jesus and the prophets. In verse sixteen, he says that "always they fill up to the brim the measure of their sins" (Amplified Bible). These are like the words of Jesus in Matthew 23. Because of the Pharisees inability to acknowledge their own weakness and need of help from Jesus, in Matthew 23:35 and 36, He again prophesies to them that all the righteous blood shed on the earth, from Abel to then, would be required of their generation. Ezekiel 18:14 says that the righteous son of a wicked man must see, consider, and discern the sin of his father. Leviticus 26:40 tells the people of God to confess our own and our father's iniquities. The Pharisees filled the measure of their fathers to overflowing by crucifying the Lord of glory.

A final concept to consider is to quantify when or if, there is a full accomplishment of healing this side of eternity. These proofs and witnesses may vary, depending on the individual and the level of affliction. In the case of the man who Jesus brought deliverance to in Luke 8:26–36, the evidence was clear and obvious. This man desired to go along with the Lord, but the Lord told him to go back home and be a witness to the compassion of the Lord. In one opportunity of ministry, the Lord Jesus had brought complete deliverance to a man who had known torment for a long time. Yet, in another instance, Jesus proclaimed the need of prayer and fasting to deliver the oppressed, although He did not pray or fast in that situation. He merely spoke the command of deliverance. Jesus carried the full anointing and flow of the Spirit without hindrance; we on the other hand, are not so sanctified. A supernatural visitation can bring this same type of immediate deliverance. The need for specific prayer and fasting for deliverance is a key factor for His disciples ministering His healing to others.

Healing, purchased by the stripes on the back of Jesus, whether physical or emotional, seems to be able to be classified under two headings. Some healings are miraculous, as in the case of the man in Luke 8. Through one time of ministry and prayer the complete healing is manifested, as also was the case in the ministry of the apostle Paul in Acts 19:11–12. The Word called these special miracles. The supernatural manifestations of special faith, gifts of healings and working of miracles all work together to powerfully bring healing to someone. Yet, healing can also come in a process, line upon line, precept upon precept. Concerning the tormented in mind or the heavily wounded, this process can be like finding hidden closet doors of the soul repeatedly. With each open door there is victory but that does not mean there are no other doors to be opened as well. This process of healing parallels the account of the healing of a blind man in Mark 8. Our ability to receive is a significant factor. Learning to trust in the goodness of God can take time as we experience His compassion through each victory. The evidence of our healing is our ability to live the overcoming life regardless of the situation or the pressures of life. A situation like the painful memory or one that had previously fueled an emotional display happens again. Do the old emotions rise and control us, or do we sense the power of God bringing a calm to our being despite the situation? Physical evidence of healing is the body performing a task it could not do before without pain or limitations. Emotional healing should be evident by an ability to live victoriously over situations that would have crippled us before.

As Zacharias prophesied many years ago, the mercy of God has been shown to us because the Dayspring from on high, the Bright and Morning Star, the Sun of righteousness, the Lord Jesus Christ, has arisen and visited His people with the healing in His wings that destroys the roots of the enemy and causes us to tread down the wicked. The reiteration of the sun arising as symbolic of this work of God declares to us that many may be walking in the darkness of their soul, but the healing work of the Sun of righteousness will cause them to come out of the darkness and into His marvelous light to which they have been called (1 Peter 2:9). Zacharias prophesied in Luke 1:78–79 that the Dayspring from on high would give light to them that sit in this darkness and in the shadow of death, thereby leading to the way of peace. Science teaches that the darkest and coldest time of the morning is the time right before dawn; the lives and memories of the wounded ring true with this statement if we parallel it to the spiritual realm. But with the sunrise comes light, warmth and renewal and God's healing Sun of righteousness can arise on behalf of His people that are oppressed and downtrodden. Believers must be willing to come out from behind the masks and coverings and stand openly in the glory of the Son. The dawning of the new day of blessing will pursue the believer if they continue in this path.

In 2 Peter 1:16–19, Peter admonishes that the testimony about the life and power of the Lord Jesus Christ was not one that he or anyone else had made up but was in fact truth. He then gives two specific witnesses for his testimony. One was the glorious scene on

Transfiguration Mountain with two other disciples, Jesus, Moses, Elijah, and Father God. Regardless of such a quantifiable experience, he gives another witness because a belief should not be solely based on an experience. The second witness is the written Word of God, the steadfast word of prophecy. Together, the glory of signs and wonders and the agreement of the written Word, are sufficient basis for a belief.

Concerning the principles and concepts of the inner healing message, many believers can testify to the manifest presence of God they have experienced during specific prayer as the brightness, the glory, and the power of the anointing of God has been seen and felt in tangible ways. Keen discernment and particular accuracies show the manifestation of the Holy Spirit to bring freedom and unlock old prisons of darkness of the soul.

Concerning the second evidence, I am persuaded that this study provides specific evidence from the Word of God that directly references many of the inner healing concepts and principles. Counseling in the realm of the Spirit is a necessary ministry in a world that is growing darker by the year. God's desire is that He could turn our mourning into dancing and that the days of mourning would be ended (Isaiah 60:20). For those who will acknowledge their own darkness, the Spirit of God calls you to an active waiting on the Lord and believing steps of faith where God has promised to arise with the provision of healing in the morning sunrise. In Psalms 119:147, it declares, "I anticipated the dawning of the morning, and cried in childlike prayer; I hoped in Your Word" (Amplified Bible). The downtrodden need to have a believing anticipation that the darkness will give way to the blast of the sunrise. Being in the grave of despair can isolate the soul, but those who look for and anticipate the dawn will be set free. God promises His help when the dawn arrives (Psalms 46:5). Even when human reason for hope is gone (Romans 4:18), the broken in heart should have assurance that He is willing and able to do what He promised. The King James word in Psalms 119:147 "prevent" means to "anticipate, to hasten, to meet for help." The church hastens with expectation the coming of the full redemption of the new heavens and the new earth (2 Peter 3:12–13), the Lord Jesus is seated at the right hand of God expecting until His enemies are made His footstool (Hebrews 10:13); therefore, we should also anticipate and do our part to bring into being the dawning of the healing Sun of righteousness into our lives and hearts. God may need to direct you to a certain fellowship or group where the Spirit is Lord and there is liberty for this type of ministry, but then we must obey and go meet Him there. God commanded Ezekiel to go into the plain and there the Lord would meet and talk with him (Ezekiel 3:22). Once planted in the place of God's direction and full of faith for the fulfillment of His promises, our childlike prayer will bring freedom to the child within us. A childlike prayer would be one of simplicity, assurance, and innocence. A child only needs a parental kiss to whisk away the pain of a scraped knee or elbow. This is the way that Father God desires us to come to Him about our heart scrapes and bruises. With our heart wide open, even with eyes full of tears, we should simply seek the kiss and intimate touch of the Holy Spirit for our wounded soul, to take away the pain and fear, that we may return to our play and activities as children of God.

Printed in the United States
by Baker & Taylor Publisher Services